LIGHTHOUSES OF FLORIDA

Help Us Keep This Guide Up to Date

Every effort has been made by the authors and editors to make this guide as accurate and useful as possible. However, many things can change after a guide is published—phone numbers change, facilities come under new management, etc.

We would love to hear from you concerning your experiences with this guide and how you feel it could be improved and be kept up to date. While we may not be able to respond to all comments and suggestions, we'll take them to heart and we'll also make certain to share them with the authors. Please send your comments and suggestions to the following address:

The Globe Pequot Press
Reader Response/Editorial Department
P. O. Box 480
Guilford, CT 06437

Or you may e-mail us at:

editorial@GlobePequot.com

Thanks for your input, and happy travels!

LIGHTHOUSES SERIES

LIGHTHOUSES OF FLORIDA

A Guidebook and Keepsake

Bruce Roberts and Ray Jones

INSIDERS' GUIDE®

GUILFORD, CONNECTICUT
AN IMPRINT OF THE GLOBE PEQUOT PRESS

INSIDERS' GUIDE®

Copyright © 2005 by Bruce Roberts and Ray Jones

All rights reserved. No part of this book may be reproduced or transmitted in any form by any means, electronic or mechanical, including photocopying and recording, or by any information storage and retrieval system, except as may be expressly permitted by the 1976 Copyright Act or by the publisher. Requests for permission should be made in writing to The Globe Pequot Press, P.O. Box 480, Guilford, Connecticut 06437.

Text design by Schwartzman Design, Deep River, CT
Map design and terrain by Stephen C. Stringall, Cartography by M.A. Dubé
Map ©The Globe Pequot Press
All photographs, unless otherwise credited, are by Bruce Roberts.

Library of Congress Cataloging-in-Publication Data
Roberts, Bruce, 1930-
    Lighthouses of Florida : a guidebook and keepsake / Bruce Roberts and Ray Jones.
  —1st ed
      p. cm. — (Lighthouses series)
    ISBN 0-7627-3736-0
      1. Lighthouses—Florida—History. 2. Lighthouses—Florida—Guidebooks
  I. Jones, Ray, 1948- II. Title III. Lighthouses series (Globe Pequot Press)

VK1024.F6R63 2005
387.1'55'09759—dc22
                        2004060889
Manufactured in China
First Edition/First Printing

The information listed in this guide was confirmed at press time. The ownership of many lighthouses, however, is gradually being transferred from the Coast Guard to private concerns. Please confirm visitor information before traveling.

DEDICATION

For Liz and Jane
—Ray Jones

For Manisha and Joy Roberts, my two granddaughters who live in
Florida. May the lights always be on for them.
—Bruce Roberts

ACKNOWLEDGMENTS

My sincerest thanks to the U.S. Coast Guard, the *Lighthouse Digest* magazine, and the American Lighthouse Foundation for their invaluable assistance with compiling the information and photographs found in this book. Many thanks also my editors and dear friends at Globe Pequot Press who have served as lights to me throughout my career. And finally, I must acknowledge Liz Taylor and Jane Austen, my two loveable and enormous Maine Coon cats who insist on climbing into my lap while I am working so they can help with the typing.

—Ray Jones

Many thanks to Bob and Sandra Shanklin (The Lighthouse People), and my friend, Mark Riddick, for contributing their photos to this book. Finally, I'd like to thank my wife, Cheryl Shelton-Roberts, who was instrumental in the making of this and so many other books.

—Bruce Roberts

CONTENTS

INTRODUCTION 1

CHAPTER ONE: AMELIA ISLAND TO HILLSBORO INLET 8
    Amelia Island Light 10
    St. Johns River Lighthouse 12
    St. Johns Light 14
    St. Augustine Light 16
    Ponce de Leon Inlet Light 18
    Cape Canaveral Light 20
    Jupiter Inlet Light 22
    Hillsboro Inlet Light 24

CHAPTER TWO: CAPE FLORIDA TO KEY WEST 26
    Cape Florida Light 30
    Fowey Rocks Light 32
    Carysfort Reef Light 34
    Alligator Reef Light 36
    Sombrero Key Light 38
    American Shoal Light 40
    Sand Key Light 42
    Key West Lighthouse 44
    Rebecca Shoal Lighthouse 46
    Garden Key Lighthouse 48
    Dry Tortugas Light 50

CHAPTER THREE: SANIBEL TO CEDAR KEY 52
    Sanibel Island Light 54
    Gasparilla Island Light 56
    Port Boca Grande Light 58
    Egmont Key Light 60
    Anclote Key Light 62
    Cedar Keys Lighthouse 64

CHAPTER FOUR: ST. MARKS TO PENSACOLA 66
    St. Marks Light 68
    Crooked River Lighthouse 70
    Dog Island Lighthouse 71
    Cape St. George Lighthouse 72
    Cape San Blas Lighthouse 74
    St. Joseph Bay Lighthouse 76
    Pensacola Light 78

GLOSSARY 80

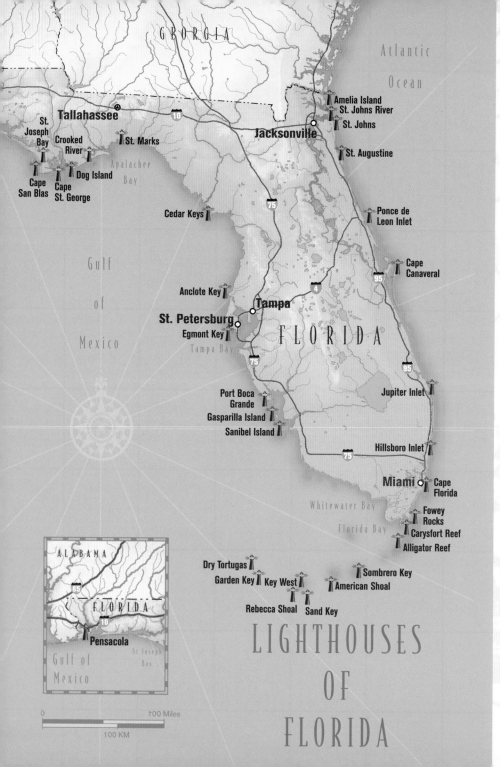

GEORGIA

Atlantic
Ocean

Tallahassee
St. Joseph Bay
Crooked River
St. Marks
Apalachee Bay
Cape San Blas
Cape St. George
Dog Island

Amelia Island
St. Johns River
St. Johns
Jacksonville
St. Augustine

Cedar Keys

Ponce de Leon Inlet

Cape Canaveral

Anclote Key

Tampa
St. Petersburg
Egmont Key
Tampa Bay

FLORIDA

Gulf

of

Mexico

Port Boca Grande
Gasparilla Island
Sanibel Island

Jupiter Inlet

Hillsboro Inlet

Miami
Cape Florida

Whitewater Bay

Florida Bay

Fowey Rocks
Carysfort Reef
Alligator Reef

Dry Tortugas
Garden Key   Key West
Rebecca Shoal   Sand Key
American Shoal
Sombrero Key

ALABAMA

FLORIDA

Pensacola

Gulf of Mexico

St. Joseph Bay

0   100 Miles

100 KM

LIGHTHOUSES

OF

FLORIDA

INTRODUCTION

Every coastal state confronts mariners with a unique set of hazards, but nowhere are they more daunting than in Florida. The long blade of the Florida peninsula extends nearly 400 miles from the southeastern corner of the North American continent, separating the Gulf of Mexico from the Atlantic and forming what is almost certainly the world's most prominent and deadly navigational obstacle. Florida's low, featureless headlands are all but invisible from the sea and the waters just offshore chock-a-block with shoals, shallows, and partially submerged barrier islands. Vessels that manage to clear the peninsula itself may yet fall prey to the Florida Keys, the 120-mile chain of wave-swept reefs and islands where, in hurricane season, entire fleets have been lost.

To help mariners deal with these dangers, Florida's shores are guarded by an extraordinarily diverse array of navigational towers. Some are skeletons of steel, while others are stout cylinders of brick or stone. Some rise from beaches at the very edge of the tides, while others stand on riverbanks or in the open ocean. Most are at least a century old, a few were built before the Civil War, and one dates all the way back to the 1820s and the years just after the United States acquired Florida from Spain. No matter when they were built, where they stand, or what they look like, however, Florida's lighthouses have a common purpose: to protect ships and save lives.

Over the years countless seamen have reached port safely thanks to the bright beacon of a Florida lighthouse, but mariners here were once completely on their own. Florida likely claimed her first vessels far back in prehistoric times. Indian traders and fishermen plied these waters in canoes, and, no doubt, faced the same perils that would later destroy much larger vessels. Who can say how many of these early Native American mariners were permanently ensnared by shoals or dumped into the surf and drowned by gales?

European explorers and the fortune-seeking conquistadors who followed them did their best to avoid Florida altogether, but that was not always possible. Those who strayed too close or were driven onto shoals by storms paid a very heavy price, and in more than a few places, Florida's coastal sands conceal the broken hulls of wooden ships—some treasure galleons, their holds stuffed with gold, silver, and jewels.

Spanish Ghost Fleets

On September 4, 1622, the Armada de Tierra Firme, a large fleet laden with precious metals and gems from the Andes, set sail from Havana bound for Spain. Before weighing anchor the fleet's wisest captains approached their admiral, the Marqués de Caderieta, and begged him not to leave the safety of the harbor. It was hurricane season, and they were acutely aware of the dangers awaiting them in the Florida Straits. Unlike his captain and their seasoned crews, however, the Marqués was not a man of the sea. A Spainish nobleman of high rank and reputation, he was anxious to impress his king by delivering this shipment of New World riches on time. A proud man, the Marqués expected absolute obedience from those who served under him, and perhaps, even from nature itself. Ignoring the desperate pleas of his men, he ordered them to sea.

The armada made good progress at first, and for two days the fleet's heavy galleons plowed steadily through the ordinarily calm straits. But on the third morning out, the sky turned dark and a strong wind blew up out of the east. The strength of the gale increased quickly, and soon helmsmen could no longer hold their ships on course. Bent over like saplings by the wind, masts snapped and tortured rudders broke loose, leaving their ships at the mercy of the storm. Driven one by one onto the Florida reefs by the relentless winds, the Marqués's ships were torn to pieces by giant waves. Off Matacumbe Key, a reef shattered the 600-ton galleon *Nuestra Señora de Atocha,* spilling her crew and more than a million pesos worth of silver bullion into the sea. Nearby, the *La Margarita* went down along with her entire crew and half a million pesos in silver. In the Dry Tortugas the galleon *Nuestra Señora del Rosario* was lost with a huge quantity of gold and tobacco. Several other vessels simply vanished along with their captains, crews, and cargoes.

In 1715, almost a century after the loss of the Armada de Tierra Firme, an even more fabulous Spanish fleet sailed from Havana— straight into the teeth of a hurricane. The fleet consisted of a dozen large ships loaded with gold, silver, South Sea pearls, Chinese porcelain, indigo, cochineal, tobacco, and rare wood. The flagship *Capitana* carried 1,300 chests filled with precious metals, and in his cabin the *Capitana*'s master kept under lock and key a special chest filled with jewels meant for the Queen of Spain. Few of these treasures would ever reach their intended destination.

Having avoided the treacherous Keys, the Armada commander shepherded his vessels into the channel separating the Florida mainland from the Bahamas, but the supposed safety of these waters would prove illusory. Soon a lookout spotted a patch of gray on the southeastern horizon, and within hours a hurricane had descended on the fleet. The powerful winds forced all but one of the twelve ships into shallows, where they were torn apart by the surf. More than 1,000 lives were lost along with most of the fleet's nearly priceless treasure.

Eight years later, a hurricane slammed into yet another Spanish treasure fleet off Florida. Comprised of twenty-two ships, many of them groaning with the weight of the gold and silver bullion in their holds, the fleet was called the Nueva España Flota. By sailing in July, Flota commander Don Rodrigo de Torres believed he would reach Spain well ahead of hurricane season, but the sea would prove him wrong. Two days after it left port the Flota ran headlong into gale-force winds blowing out of the north. Torres tried to hurry the fleet back to Havana, but the wind soon swung around to the south, pushing inexorably toward the Keys. By nightfall all twenty-two ships had wrecked. The total loss in treasure has never been calculated, but just two of the wrecked vessels, the *El Rubi* and *El Gallo* held cargoes with an estimated combined value of more than nine million pesos. No one knows how many lives were lost.

Florida Lights Up

Despite the incalculable losses suffered by the Spanish along the Florida coast, there is no clear evidence that they ever built light-houses here. Construction of effective maritime aids would be left to the United States, which took possession of Florida in 1821. The United States could ill afford to be as lax as the Spanish had been since the nation's livelihood increasingly depended on safe navigation of the Florida Straits. Following the Louisiana Purchase in 1803, the seas around Florida had become the young nation's busiest commercial highway. Since the great wall of the Appalachian Mountains divided the rich farm and cattle lands of the Mississippi Basin from the populous cities of the East Coast, western produce had to be shipped to market by sea. Timber, grain, and livestock were floated down the big, muddy Mississippi River in flatboats to New Orleans and then shipped to the U.S. Atlantic coast or Europe.

The voyage invariably took merchant ships around the southern tip of the Florida peninsula, and every year Florida and its Keys exacted a toll on ships, crews, and cargoes. Wrecks occurred with such regularity that salvaging lost cargo became a major industry. A thriving town, almost entirely supported by the salvaging business, took root on Key West. There, dozens of salvaging crews, called "wreckers," worked year-round pulling bales of cotton, loads of lumber, and other valuable goods from the smashed hulls of ships that had run aground off Florida.

Clearly, an adequate system of navigational lights was needed here, and U.S. maritime authorities declared their intention to mark Florida "from end to end" with a continuous "band of light." The first Florida lighthouse, a 65-foot tower at Key West, was built in 1825. By the following year similar lighthouses stood on Garden Key, Sand Key, Cape Florida, and the Dry Tortugas, about 70 miles west of Key West. In the decades that followed, lights also appeared at the mouth of the St. Johns River, Amelia Island, Cape Canaveral, and Jupiter Inlet.

Ironically, the Florida lighthouses were themselves only a little safer than the ships they guided. Even more exposed than their cousins on the rocky shores of New England or the sandy barrier islands of the Carolinas, they lay under constant threat of gale and hurricane. But wind and high water were not the only threats they faced. During the 1830s war repeatedly darkened the Florida coast as Seminole Indians fought to hold back the tidal wave of white farmers and ranchers washing over their lands. Settlements all over the peninsula came under attack by Seminole war parties, and isolated lighthouses proved particularly vulnerable.

Burned by Indians

Late in 1835, Seminole warriors descended on a recently built lighthouse at Mosquito Inlet just south of what is now Daytona Beach and set the tower on fire. The station had been damaged almost beyond repair by a storm while still under construction, and the Indians now completed its destruction. Soon after the fires died down, the tower toppled into the sea.

A few months later on Key Biscayne, the Seminoles raided the Cape Florida Light, killing the keeper's wife and children. Although he survived the attack, the keeper was so distraught over the loss of his family that he abandoned his post and never again set foot in a light-house. A new keeper was appointed, a man named John Thompson, and by summer 1836 he had begun to believe the Indian threat had subsided. He was wrong.

On the afternoon of July 23, 1836, Thompson stepped through the kitchen door of the Cape Florida keeper's residence just as several Indian war canoes were pulling onto the nearby beach. Thompson shouted a warning to his assistant, Henry, and the two ran as fast as they could to the station's fortresslike, brick tower. They had barely enough time to bar the door before the pursuing Seminoles piled up against it.

Thompson and Henry drove their attackers back with muskets, but the Seminoles replied with musket fire of their own, peppering the brick walls, splintering the door, and perforating a tin storage tank containing 225 gallons of lamp oil. Streams of oil squirted through the holes, soaking the floor and walls. Flaming arrows then set fire to the door, which, in turn, ignited the oil.

With flames hot at their heels, the defenders retreated up the wooden tower steps. Once at the top they tried in vain to cut away the steps so the merciless Seminoles could not follow, but the fire soon did the job for them, turning the tower into a giant torch. Thompson and Henry took refuge in the lantern, which was constructed mainly of iron, but the metal was already scorching hot. Both men realized, in horror, that they were about to be roasted alive.

"At last the awful moment arrived," Thompson wrote in his account of the attack. "The crackling flames burst around me. The savages at the same time began their hellish yells. Henry looked at me with tears in his eyes, but he could not speak."

Once more Thompson and Henry tried to escape the fire, this time by climbing out onto the narrow, metal platform surrounding the gallery. There they lay flat on their bellies to avoid being shot by the Seminoles, who still had their muskets ready. "The lantern was now full of flame," said Thompson, "the lamps and glasses bursting and flying in all directions."

The iron beneath the men grew so hot that they could no longer bear the pain of touching it. Thompson had brought a musket and a keg of gunpowder with him to the lantern. He now jumped up and threw the keg down into the burning lighthouse. He meant to blow up the tower and put himself and his friend out of their misery, taking, he hoped, a few of the hated Seminoles along with him. With a tremendous roar the keg exploded, rocking the tower. But, said Thompson, "it had not the desired effect of blowing me into eternity." Instead, the explosion knocked out the flames.

By this time Henry was already dead. No longer able to lie on the sizzling gallery floor, he had tried to stand and was cut down by a Seminole musket ball. Although the fire had died down, Thompson thought of jumping off the tower and joining his friend in death. "I was almost as bad off as before," he said, "a burning fever on me, my feet shot to pieces, no clothes to cover me, nothing to eat or drink, a hot sun overhead, a dead man by my side, no friend near or any to expect, and placed between seventy and eighty feet from the earth with no chance of getting down."

Unknown to Thompson, help *was* on the way. Sailors on the U.S. Navy schooner *Concord* had heard the explosion, and the warship soon dropped anchor in the bay within sight of the ruined lighthouse. A detachment of marines and seamen from the *Concord* landed a short time afterward and found that the Seminoles had departed. They also discovered, much to their surprise, that the lighthouse keeper had survived the attack. There he was in the lantern, waving at them and calling for help. But how were they to get him down? First they tried to fly a line to Thompson with a kite. When this failed, they tied the line to a ramrod and fired it up into the lantern with a musket. Employing the last of his strength, Thompson used the line to pull up a block and tackle, enabling two sailors to hoist themselves along the outer tower walls to the gallery. Carefully lowered to the ground, the half-dead keeper was soon on his way to a military hospital for treatment of his burns and wounds. Thompson recovered and later continued his service as a lighthouse keeper. He had survived his worst on-the-job experience; not all Florida keepers would be so fortunate.

How to Use This Guide

Florida's lighthouses have many fascinating stories to tell, not all of them as grim as that of the Seminole raid on Cape Florida. In *Lighthouses of Florida* you will read about the near miraculous construction of open-ocean towers in the Florida Keys, the mysterious destruction of lighthouses in the Florida panhandle, the ingenious U.S. Army engineer who built several of Florida's most extraordinary light towers and then led the Union to victory at Gettysburg. Read the stories, learn the facts, and then stake your claim to a share of America's rich maritime heritage by going to visit a Florida lighthouse.

Florida boasts more than thirty standing light towers and every one is worth a look. This book takes you to each accessible lighthouse and to some that simply can't be reached. It also takes a loving backward glance at Florida's "Lost Lights," beacons that once shined bright but were snuffed out long ago.

The book is divided into four sections: Amelia Island to Hillsboro Inlet; Cape Florida to Key West; Sanibel to Cedar Key; and St. Marks to Pensacola. Within each section lighthouses are presented geographically. This arrangement should make it easier to plan your own Florida lighthouse outings—so should the directions, telephone contacts, and other travel information included at the end of each listing.

Under normal circumstances you should be able to visit the most attractive and historic lighthouses in one or another of the sections mentioned above in a single, long-weekend excursion. To help you select the lighthouses you want to visit, individual listings include advice in the form of simple symbols: ▣ for lighthouses that are especially historic—most of them are; ⌨ for lighthouses that are accessible by car, boat, or foot—more than a few are not; ✍ for visitor-friendly lighthouses that are frequently open to the public and feature museums or similar attractions; ⌾ for lighthouses that make great pictures—most of them are quite photogenic; and ⌂ for lighthouses that are no longer standing. For added convenience every listing also includes an easy-to-read summary of key information on the lighthouse: location; date the light was established (placed in operation); tower height; elevation of the focal plane; type of optic; current status; characteristic; range; and, for all active lighthouses, the precise latitude and longitude of the beacon.

We hope you enjoy your Florida lighthouse adventure.

CHAPTER ONE:
AMELIA ISLAND TO HILLSBORO INLET

D uring the mid-nineteenth century, the U.S. Lighthouse Board launched one of the boldest government projects in U.S. history—the construction of a 1,000-mile-long chain of colossal navigational towers along the southern coast. Begun shortly before the Civil War and completed over a period of several decades, this procession of giants included what were then some of the loftiest man-made structures on the planet. The tallest and best known of these soaring sentinels is the 191-foot spiral-striped Cape Hatteras tower on North Carolina's Outer Banks, but there are more twenty others spaced an average of about 40 miles apart from the mouth of the Chesapeake to Miami.

More than a third of the chain's length—some 400 miles—stretches along the east coast of Florida, and several of its most impressive towers can be found there. Just south of Daytona Beach, a redbrick goliath raises its lantern 175 feet above Ponce de Leon Inlet. Built in 1874, it still guides mariners with a bright beacon focused by a classic prismatic lens. Almost as tall is the 167-foot tower that serves the old Spanish port of St. Augustine. Its huge, first-order Fresnel lens, in use since 1874, is one of the last of its kind in America. And, not far from the NASA launch pads at the Kennedy Space Center, stands another colossus, the 150-foot brick and iron Cape Canaveral tower. It is said that during the 1950s and 1960s scientists sometimes climbed the tower to watch rocket launchings from its lantern room.

Florida's east coast lighthouses are remarkable not just because of their height but also because of their considerable age. Some are even older than the state they serve. For instance, the Amelia Island tower near Fernandina Beach dates back to before the United States acquired Florida from the Spanish. Like many Florida residents today, it is an immigrant rather than a native. Built in 1820, it stood on Georgia's Little Cumberland Island for nearly twenty years before being dismantled, shipped south, and reassembled on Amelia Island. The St. Augustine station dates to 1824 and the St. Johns River station to 1830. The Jupiter Inlet Light north of Miami was built in 1860 just before the Civil War. Interestingly, Robert E. Lee surveyed the site for the Jupiter Inlet Light and George Meade helped design its tower. Later on, these two army engineers would face off against one another as opposing commanders at the battle of Gettysburg.

AMELIA ISLAND LIGHT

I n 1820 the government had a 50-foot tower erected on Georgia's Cumberland Island to mark the mouth of the St. Marys River, which forms a natural border between Georgia and Florida. Following the annexation of Florida in 1821 by the United States, maritime officials decided the lighthouse would provide better service on the south bank of the river. So, in 1839, the tower was dismantled and moved to Amelia Island in Florida. There it was reassembled on a piece of land the government had purchased from a local plantation owner. The height of the tower was raised by at least 14 feet as part of its reconstruction.

Amelia Island Light is a classic Victorian structure with a tapering whitewashed stone tower and a gleaming black lantern as a crown. The tower was given an unusual stairway made of granite shipped from quarries in New England. Several times each night the keeper climbed its sixty-eight steps in order to tend the clockwork mechanism that drove the rotating classical lens. The keeper "rewound" the device by raising heavy weights that dropped through the center of the tower.

A third-order Fresnel lens placed here in 1903 still shines each night, displaying a flashing light. Navigators approaching the dangerous shoals in nearby Nassau Sound see a white flash, while others see a red flash.

Upkeep of this historic lighthouse has been placed in the hands of the City of Fernandina Beach. In 2002 the city received a $350,000 grant to restore the lighthouse. The work is now complete, and the tower and other station structures returned to like-new condition.

TO SEE THE LIGHT: Used as a private residence for Coast Guard personnel, the lighthouse is closed to the public. The tower can be seen and photographed from Highway A1A and Atlantic Avenue in Old Fernandina Beach. However, the romantically inclined may prefer to enjoy this historic lighthouse by taking an evening walk along one of Amelia Island's lovely beaches and watching the warm, reassuring flash of the beacon.

Location: Fernandina Beach

Established: 1839

Tower height: 64 feet

Elevation of the focal plane: 107 feet

Optic: Fresnel lens (third order)

Status: Active

Characteristic: Flashes every 10 seconds (red sector)

Range: 23 miles

Position: 30° 40' 24
81° 26' 30

Note: Tower moved here from Georgia's Little Cumberland Island

ST. JOHNS RIVER LIGHTHOUSE

N ow a bustling thoroughfare for commercial freighters, fishing boats, and pleasure craft, the St. Johns River was once an untamed frontier. Its first navigational light was likely a simple oil lamp hung on a pole. The river's first official lighthouse was completed in 1830 at a cost of $24,000—a considerable sum at the time. But despite its hefty price tag, the structure lasted little more than five years. Surging tides quickly undermined its foundation, and it was torn down in 1835. That same year a second lighthouse was built, but by the early 1850s nearby sand dunes had piled up so high that the beacon could no longer be seen from the sea.

Completed in 1859, the river's third lighthouse was a 66-foot brick tower fitted with a third-order Fresnel lens. Its lamps burned regularly until 1864, when Confederate gunners shot out the light in hopes of blinding federal gunboats. The light was quickly restored following the Civil War. In 1887 brick masons added 15 feet to the tower, raising it to a height of 81 feet. The light served until 1929, when a lightship moored 7 miles from the mouth of the St. Johns replaced it. The old tower remains in excellent shape, although almost 20 feet of it is now underground. It was buried during construction of a runway for the adjacent Mayport Naval Station.

TO SEE THE LIGHT: Follow Highway A1A to Mayport Naval Station. If traveling south on A1A, you may need to take the St. Johns River Ferry that crosses to Mayport every thirty minutes; for ferry information call (904) 246–2922. The lighthouse can be seen from Broad Street, just outside the air station, but as of this writing the base itself is closed due to security considerations. For current status and other information, contact the Public Affairs Office, Mayport Naval Station, P.O. Box 280032, Mayport, 32228 or call (904) 270–5226.

Location: Mayport

Established: 1830

Tower height: 81 feet

Elevation of the focal plane: 77 feet

Optic: Fresnel lens (third order) removed

Status: Deactivated in 1929

Note: Lower portion of the tower was buried during construction of a runway

Built in 1830, this red-brick, torch-shaped tower is all that remains of one of Florida's earliest lighthouses. While the structure is still in good condition, it has not been used for navigational purposes since 1929.

ST. JOHNS LIGHT

J ust south of the entrance to Florida's strategic
and commercially vital St. Johns River stands
one of the most unusual lighthouses in America.
The St. Johns Light has an angular, modern
appearance, in no way suggestive of a traditional,
cone-shaped light tower. Perhaps not surprisingly,
the structure is relatively young by lighthouse stan-
dards. It was built in 1954, at about the time Elvis
Presley launched his career.

Unlike most other lighthouses, the 67-foot St.
Johns tower has no lantern room. Instead, it has a
flat roof with a revolving, airport-style optic resting
on top like a hat that's far too small for it. Despite
its appearance, this is a powerful light, producing
a beacon that can be seen from nearly 20 miles
away. The St. Johns beacon guides mighty aircraft
carriers and other U.S. Navy fighting ships in and
out of the harbor.

In 1942, about a dozen years before the lighthouse was built, a German submarine slipped into
the mouth of the St. Johns River under cover of
darkness and dropped off a team of Nazi spies.
Four German agents came ashore in a rubber boat
not far from where the tower now stands, moved
on to Jacksonville, and waited there for word of a
second undercover team that had landed on Long
Island. They waited in vain. Neither group managed
to do any damage as they were soon rounded up
by the FBI. In time all were tried for espionage and
either sentenced to prison or executed.

TO SEE THE LIGHT: Located on an active military
base, the lighthouse is off-limits to the public. Its
light can be seen from the waters off Jacksonville.

Location: Mayport

Established: 1954

Tower height: 67 feet

Elevation of the focal
plane: 83 feet

Optic: Modern

Status: Active

Characteristic: Flashes
four times every
20 seconds

Range: 19 miles

Position: 30° 23' 06
81° 23' 54

Note: Nazi spies landed
near here in 1942

ST. AUGUSTINE LIGHT

S hortly after the United States acquired Florida from Spain in 1821, a federal customs collector placed a lantern in an old stone tower to guide American ships to St. Augustine. A more conventional 73-foot brick tower soon replaced this rather primitive lighthouse, but its weak reflecting light could be seen from only a short distance beyond the harbor entrance. Although darkened during the Civil War, the St. Augustine Light survived the conflict—only to be flattened by tidal erosion. Before the tower collapsed, however, the government established a new light station on nearby Anastasia Island. The keeper lit the lamps inside its first-order Fresnel lens on October 15, 1874. From atop this new, 167-foot brick tower, a combination fixed and flashing light shot its beam through some 24 miles of darkness. Painted in distinctive black-and-white barber-pole stripes, the tower helps guide mariners during the day, as well.

In 1986 a bizarre incidence of vandalism almost destroyed the station's priceless first-order Fresnel lens. A fourteen-year-old armed with a high-powered rifle took aim and fired directly into the lantern, shattering many of the glass prisms that focus the station's beacon. Fashioned and polished to perfection in Paris during the nineteenth century, the delicate crystal prisms were terribly difficult and expensive to replace. Repairs were successfully completed, however, with $500,000 raised by the Junior Service League.

TO SEE THE LIGHT: In St. Augustine follow Highway A1A and Old Beach Road to Lighthouse Avenue. The beautifully restored brick keeper's residence houses an excellent museum that celebrates the history of the lighthouse and coastal Florida. For a gull's-eye view of the Atlantic and the old Spanish town of St. Augustine, visitors may climb the 219 steps to the service gallery. Contact the St. Augustine Lighthouse and Museum, 81 Lighthouse Avenue, St. Augustine, 32084; call (904) 829–0745.

Location: St. Augustine

Established: 1824

Tower height: 167 feet

Elevation of the focal plane: 161 feet

Optic: Fresnel lens (first order)

Status: Active

Characteristic: Fixed with one flash every 30 seconds

Range: 24 miles

Position: 29° 53' 08 81° 17' 19

Note: In 1986 historic lens was shot out by a young vandal armed with a high-powered rifle

The broad, black-and-white stripes of St. Augustine tower help mariners distinguish it from other tall structures along the northeast Florida coast. Also distinctive is its red lantern containing a giant first-order Fresnel lens.

PONCE DE LEON INLET LIGHT

The first lighthouse built for Ponce de Leon Inlet, then called Mosquito Inlet, collapsed before its lamps had ever been lit. Oil for the lamps had not been delivered in 1835 when a storm undermined the tower's foundation. Hostile Seminoles prevented laborers from rescuing the tower from further damage, and it soon fell over. Afterward, discouraged maritime officials decided to abandon the project.

More than fifty years would pass before another lighthouse was built here, this time on the north side of what is now known as Ponce de Leon Inlet. Using high quality brick shipped from Baltimore, workers erected a 175-foot tower, the second tallest on the East Coast. Lit in autumn 1887, the flashing Ponce de Leon Lighthouse helped fill the 95-mile gap between the St. Augustine Light approximately 50 miles to the north and the Cape Canaveral Light about 50 miles to the south.

This lighthouse served all sorts of traffic, including Bahama-bound, Prohibition-era rumrunners, who often pulled into the inlet at night to avoid trouble on the reefs. It was taken out of service in 1970, however, because the beacon atop the New Smyrna Coast Guard Station made it redundant. However, the old light stayed out of service only for a little more than a dozen years: It was reinstated in 1983 when a sprouting condominium development obscured the New Smyrna beacon.

TO SEE THE LIGHT: Its tower, dwellings, and other outbuildings beautifully restored, the light station complex comprises one of the finest lighthouse museums in America. A special exhibit building houses an enormous first-order, clamshell-type Fresnel lens that once served at Cape Canaveral. Contact the Ponce de Leon Inlet Lighthouse Museum, 4931 South Peninsula Drive, Ponce Inlet, 32127; call (386) 761-1821.

Location: Ponce Inlet

Established: 1887

Tower height: 175 feet

Elevation of the focal plane: 164 feet

Optic: Fresnel lens (third order)

Status: Active

Characteristic: Flashes six times every 15 seconds

Range: 22 miles

Position: 29° 04' 48 80° 55' 42

Note: One of the nation's best lighthouse museums

The big, red-brick tower at Ponce de Leon Inlet is part of a delightful maritime museum featuring one of the first displays of lighthouses in America. The tower houses a still-functioning third-order Fresnel lens.

CAPE CANAVERAL LIGHT

Thrusting eastward into the Atlantic, Cape Canaveral poses a formidable threat to ships moving along the Florida peninsula. Yet when the government marked the cape with a 65-foot brick tower in 1848, it may have done more harm than good. The light proved so weak that captains often ran their vessels aground on nearby shoals while searching for the signal. The Civil War cut short efforts to correct this unhappy situation.

After the war, the U.S. Lighthouse Board gave the Cape Canaveral station high priority. They constructed a cast-iron cylinder tower fitted with a first-order Fresnel lens. Shining from atop the 150-foot, brick-lined tower, the light could be seen from 24 miles away, a distance sufficient to keep ships away from the shoals. In 1893 beach erosion forced relocation of the lighthouse to a new site about a mile inland.

A modern, automated beacon replaced the massive glass Fresnel lens in 1993. Sailors still use the light to navigate safely around the Canaveral shoals, but nowadays the cape is lit with even brighter lights as rockets rush skyward from the Kennedy Space Center.

TO SEE THE LIGHT: Located on an active Air Force base, the lighthouse is off-limits to casual visitors. However, it can be seen from the nearby Kennedy Space Center. Contact Spaceport U.S.A./Visitor Center, Kennedy Space Center, 32899; call (321) 452-2121. Guided bus tours of the center and the adjacent Cape Canaveral Air Station provide the best views of the lighthouse; call (312) 449-4444.

Location: Cape Canaveral

Established: 1848

Tower height: 150 feet

Elevation of the focal plane: 137 feet

Optic: Modern

Status: Active

Characteristic: Flashes twice every 20 seconds

Range: 24 miles

Position: 28° 27' 37
          80° 32' 36

Note: Stands within sight of rocket launchings at Kennedy Space Center

Scientists have often stood in the lofty Cape Canaveral Lighthouse lantern to watch rocket launchings at the nearby Kennedy Space Center. Ironically, satellites hurled into orbit from the cape have ushered in the era of pinpoint electronic navigation and so diminished the need for lighthouses. Photo courtesy of NASA

JUPITER INLET LIGHT

R obert E. Lee surveyed the site for the Jupiter Inlet Light station, and George Meade designed and supervised construction of the 125-foot Jupiter tower. Ironically, the two U.S. Army engineers who made the Jupiter lighthouse possible would square off against each other during the famous Civil War battle at Gettysburg, with General Meade emerging the victor.

The Jupiter Inlet Light itself played a role in the Civil War. Established just prior to the fratricidal conflict that plunged much of America into darkness, it had burned for little more than a year before being snuffed out by Confederate raiders. Following the war, keeper James Armour found the station's first-order Fresnel lens hidden in a creek. He soon restored the lens to its proper place in the Jupiter Inlet tower and had the light back in operation by the end of 1866. The big lens remains in use to this day.

The lighthouse has been battered by nature as well as war. A 1928 hurricane knocked out both the primary and emergency electric power, forcing keeper Charles Seabrook to reinstall the station's old mineral lamps. When the keeper fell ill from exhaustion, his sixteen-year-old son climbed the swaying tower steps to rotate the lens by hand and keep the light flashing.

Although a sign in front of the lighthouse says, IT HAS NOT MISSED A NIGHT IN OVER 100 YEARS, the light was, in fact, darkened briefly in the 1950s when a hurricane knocked out the windows in the lantern and smashed the irreplaceable bull's-eye lens. This misfortune might have doomed the light had not technician James Maher painstakingly cemented the shards back into their original configuration and bound them together with a brass frame.

In 1973 the Jupiter Inlet Light was placed on the National Register of Historic Places.

TO SEE THE LIGHT: Open to the public as a key attraction of the nearby Florida History Center and Museum, the bright red tower is located in Jupiter Lighthouse Park, reached via Highway 707 off U.S. Highway 1; call (561) 747–8380. The museum is in Burt Reynolds Park, off U.S. Highway 1 in Jupiter. Contact the Florida History Center and Museum, 805 North U.S. Highway One, Jupiter, 33477; call (561) 747–6639.

Location: Jupiter

Established: 1860

Tower height: 125 feet

Elevation of the focal plane: 146 feet

Optic: Fresnel lens (first order)

Status: Active

Characteristic: Flashes twice every 30 seconds

Range: 25 miles

Position: 26° 56' 55
80° 04' 55

Note: During the Civil War, Confederates hid the lens in a creek

HILLSBORO INLET LIGHT

L ooming dramatically above Hillsboro Inlet near Pompano Beach, this cast-iron skeleton tower fits right into the local scenery, but it is not a Florida native. A Chicago foundry fabricated the 137-foot tower, and it was barged down the Mississippi to St. Louis, where it delighted crowds at the 1904 St. Louis Exposition. After the fair the government bought the lighthouse, took it apart, and reassembled it on faraway Hillsboro Inlet in Florida. The second-order Fresnel lens, purchased by the U.S. Lighthouse Service in 1907 for $90,000, still functions, displaying a flashing white light with an impressive range of 28 miles. The light marks the northern approaches to Miami.

The last major seacoast lighthouse erected in Florida, the Hillsboro Inlet tower was built to last. Anchored by six huge iron legs, the iron-skeleton structure was designed to allow gale force winds to pass through harmlessly. The tower's white-and-black paint job made it easily distinguishable from the redbrick lighthouses at Jupiter Inlet and Cape Florida.

The station's light was produced by kerosene lamps, which required frequent tending by keepers who had to climb the 175 steps that wound upward through the central steel cylinder. The light was converted to electric power during the late 1920s.

TO SEE THE LIGHT: Located on an active Coast Guard facility near Pompano Beach, the lighthouse is not usually open to the public. It can be viewed or photographed from the Highway A1A bridge over Hillsboro Inlet or from the beach on the south shore.

Location: Pompano Beach

Established: 1907

Tower height: 137 feet

Elevation of the focal plane: 136 feet

Optic: Fresnel lens (second order)

Status: Active

Characteristic: Flashes white every 30 seconds

Range: 28 miles

Position: 26° 15' 33
80° 04' 51

Note: The tower first served as an exhibit at the 1904 St. Louis Exposition

CHAPTER TWO:
CAPE FLORIDA TO KEY WEST

Probably no mariner has ever been happier to see a shore light than Christopher Columbus. One night more than 500 years ago, the explorer peered into the darkness and caught his first glimpse of the New World—the light of a fire dancing on the western horizon. If there was fire, then there was also land, and he would soon find it.

Perhaps the closest we can come to the Columbus experience nowadays is to drive Florida's aptly named Overseas Highway. Linking the southern tip of the Florida peninsula with Key West, this unique roadway reaches more than 130 miles out into the ocean. For long stretches between the low, sandy keys, it spans the open blue-green water. Dolphins and seabirds play in the waves only a few feet from the concrete. Motorists begin to feel like mariners and at night, especially, may imagine they are about to drop off the edge of the earth. Helping to restore their confidence are the navigational lights at Carysfort Reef, Alligator Reef, Sombrero Key, American Shoal, and Sand Key, winking at them all along the way.

The reef lighthouses of the Florida Keys are like few other navigational towers anywhere on the planet. Designed and built during the nineteenth century, they represented the highest technology and finest engineering the scientifically oriented Victorian era had to offer. The clear thinking and hard work devoted to them has paid huge dividends as these open-water towers still stand and remain in operation today, more than 125 years after the last of them was built. During more than a century of service, the Florida reef towers have saved innumerable lives while standing tall through history's worst gales and hurricanes.

A pair of lighthouses just below Miami at the far northeastern end of the Keys provide a fascinating and instructive comparison. One of Florida's oldest navigational towers, the all-brick Cape Florida Lighthouse was built on land at Key Biscayne in 1825. Half a century later it was rendered obsolete by the iron-skeleton Fowey Rocks Light built in the open ocean just a few miles south of the cape. Those who built this "Eiffel Tower of the Atlantic" in 1878 drew on designs and techniques pioneered at earlier reef light construction sights, and what they accomplished signified not just a move from land to water, but a whole new way of thinking.

In 1825 one of the nation's first lightships was placed on station at Carysfort Reef, a few miles off Key Largo. This notorious obstacle

The original brick tower
of the Cape Florida Light.

was named for a shipwreck, that of the British frigate *Carysford* (the "d" was later replaced with a "t"), lost on the reef along with most of her crew in 1770. The reef had destroyed many earlier vessels and, after the *Carysford* disaster, continued to ruin ships at such a rate that several crews of wreckers earned a good living by salvaging their broken remains. Built in New York the previous year, the *Carysfort Lightship* sailed southward toward the Keys, but short of its destination took an ignominious detour: The lightship slammed into a reef before reaching the one it was supposed to mark. When the crew abandoned ship, a party of unscrupulous salvagers took possession of the vessel and sailed it to Key West, where they put it up for sale. The U.S. government was then forced to buy back its own ship for $10,000.

After finally reaching Carysfort Reef, the lightship's service record continued to be spotty. Its time on station was constantly interrupted by storms that tore it from its anchors, sometimes driving it aground on the very reef it was intended to guard; by Indians, who attacked crewmen when they went ashore for supplies; and even by its own rotten timbers, which finally put it out of service for good only five years after it was launched. A second ship replaced the original *Carysfort Lightship* in 1830, and this one served until 1852, when an entirely new concept of marking the Florida Keys came into being.

Many of the lighthouses built in the early nineteenth century were the work of Winslow Lewis, designer of a well-known lamp-and-reflector system for navigational lights. Ironically, Lewis's own nephew was destined to become his chief critic. A government contractor himself, I. W. P. Lewis found fault with his uncle's brick-and-mortar designs for light towers as well as his vaunted lamp-and-reflector optic, described by some disgruntled mariners as "little more than an ordinary barnyard lantern held in front of a mirror."

Unlike his uncle, the younger Lewis saw merit in the sophisti-cated, though expensive, Fresnel lenses manufactured and sold by the French. Likewise he was intrigued by the recently developed screw-pile technique for open-water construction and by the possi-bility of substituting steel for masonry when building lighthouses. He thought these new ideas might make it possible to erect lighthouses directly over the most dangerous reefs and shoals in the Florida Keys. At Carysfort Reef Lewis would finally get the chance to put his fresh approach to a rigorous test.

Built less than a decade before the outbreak of the American Civil War, the Carysfort Reef Lighthouse was the product of a nation caught in a tide of revolutionary change. A 110-foot skeleton of braced-steel supports firmly anchored to massive iron pilings, it was a radical departure from traditional light towers of brick, stone, or wood. Indeed, Winslow Lewis, who had built many of those earlier lighthouses, also submitted a bid for construction of an open-water tower at Carysfort Reef. His design called for a conical tower with solid walls of blocked stone resting on a massive caisson. A special government panel rejected the plan, however, opting instead for one put forward by the contractor's nephew.

One of the first of its kind, the lighthouse stood—and still stands, almost a century and a half after it was built—on eight cast-iron legs arranged in an octagon some 50 feet wide. Each leg was anchored to the sea bottom by means of a screw pile, a hollow, iron shaft with an auger-like bit that was twisted at least 10 feet down through the coral and underlying sand. To stabilize the piles laborers capped them with massive iron discs 4 feet in diameter.

Braced by iron girders and tie bars, the legs held aloft a 24-foot-wide platform on which a two-story keeper's dwelling was built. A second platform about 100 feet above the water held the lantern. Keepers reached the lantern room by way of a staircase rising through a cylinder centered between the outer piles. I. W. P. Lewis saw to it that the lantern was fitted with a high-quality, first-order Fresnel lens—and not a reflector-style lighting system similar to the one his uncle had invented. Lighted by a whale-oil lamp, the lens emitted flashes seen from up to 15 miles away.

Today, the Carysfort Reef Light has an electric lamp powered by batteries, which in turn are recharged by solar panels. Ships passing the reefs rely on radar and navigational information relayed to them by satellites far more than on the guidance offered by lighthouse beacons. Naturally, the advance of navigational technology did not stop with construction of the Florida reef lighthouses, but it did take a mighty leap forward. Vacationers driving to Key West may gaze out toward the flashing lights on the horizons and know they are seeing not just lighthouse beacons but bright markers along the road of human progress.

CAPE FLORIDA LIGHT

A Seminole war party swooped down on the Cape Florida Lighthouse in 1836, killing the keeper's assistant and torching the tower. Keeper John Thompson survived by retreating to the lantern room, 60 feet above ground, as the tower steps below him went up in flames. The fortuitous arrival of a U.S. Navy warship saved the badly burned Thompson from certain death by starvation or exposure.

The threat of Indian attack made repair of the lighthouse impossible for nearly a decade. Despite the fire and a decade of neglect, the original hollow-walled brick tower remained standing, however. After raising the height of the tower to 95 feet, government restoration crews had the station back in operation by the end of 1846.

Restored once again in 1866, the station served another twelve years, after which it was replaced by an offshore lighthouse at Fowey Rocks, about 2 miles southeast of Key Biscayne. But the story of the Cape Florida Light did not end there. After its light was extinguished in 1878, the tower languished dark and empty for a century—more than twice as long as it had served as an active aid to navigation. The old tower might have been demolished or fallen over during a hurricane, but fortunately for lighthouse and history buffs, it still stands. In fact it has been handsomely refurbished, thanks to $1.5 million in privately donated and state-matching funds.

TO SEE THE LIGHT: The lighthouse is located on Key Biscayne, southeast of downtown Miami. From I-95 follow the Rickenbacker (toll) Causeway and Crandon Boulevard. Contact Bill Baggs Cape Florida State Park, 1200 South Crandon Boulevard, Key Biscayne, 33149; call (305) 361-5811.

Location: Key Biscayne

Established: 1836

Tower height: 95 feet

Elevation of the focal plane: 95 feet

Optic: Modern

Status: Active

Characteristic: Flashes every 6 seconds

Range: 20 miles

Position: 25° 40' 00
80° 09' 24

Note: Attacked at least twice by Seminole Indians

Decommissioned in 1878, the Cape Florida Lighthouse stood abandoned and at the mercy of hurricanes for a century. Although returned to operation in 1978, the weathered tower remained at risk. Increased interest in historic structures in general and lighthouses in particular led to a complete restoration during the late 1990s. Mark Riddick

FOWEY ROCKS LIGHT

The Fowey Rocks shoal took its name from the HMS *Fowey*, a British Navy frigate that ran aground there in 1748, with tragic results. The ship was lost along with most of her crew. Over the years many other hapless vessels followed the *Fowey* to their doom on this murderous reef.

Aware that the Cape Florida Light failed to give adequate warning of the shoal, the U.S. Lighthouse Board decided to establish a light station directly over Fowey Rocks. It was a bold undertaking since the lighthouse would have to be built in open water in a region frequented by raging gales and killer hurricanes.

When completed, the Fowey Rocks tower stood 110 feet tall, its spidery iron legs firmly anchored to the hard, subsurface coral reef. The tower was built on eight pilings, driven not just into the coral, but through massive iron discs resting on a stabilized concrete foundation. The iron skeleton superstructure that rests atop the foundation exposes a minimum of surface to destructive winds. This arrangement has proven so durable that the tower has survived for more than 125 years, during which time countless ferocious hurricanes and gales have swept over the station.

Keepers reached the lantern room by way of a spiral staircase inside the central, steel cylinder. There a first-order Fresnel lens flashed out an alternating white and red warning beacon. Before it was installed at the Fowey Rocks station, the big Fresnel had fascinated crowds at the U.S. Lighthouse Service exhibit at the 1876 Philadelphia Centennial Exposition. The huge lens served until the station was automated in 1974, when it was replaced by a high-powered modern optic.

TO SEE THE LIGHT: Rising from open water more than 10 miles south of Key Biscayne, the Fowey Rocks Lighthouse can be seen very distantly from the shore near the Cape Florida Lighthouse; the best way to see it, though, is from the water. The lighthouse is now part of Biscayne National Park. For more information on the park and boating in the vicinity of the lighthouse, call (305) 230–7275.

Location: Southeast of
Key Biscayne

Established: 1878

Tower height: 110 feet

Elevation of the focal
plane: 110 feet

Optic: Modern
(solar powered)

Status: Active

Characteristic: Flashes
every 10 seconds
(red sector)

Range: 15 miles

Position: 25° 35' 24
80° 05' 48

Note: Has been described
as the "Eiffel Tower of
the Atlantic"

CARYSFORT REEF LIGHT

The 110-foot, iron-skeleton Carysfort Reef tower represented a completely new approach to lighthouse construction. Legendary contractor Winslow Lewis, who built so many of the nation's early masonry light towers, submitted a bid to erect this one, using familiar stone-construction techniques. Officials opted instead for a more radical plan put forward by I. W. P. Lewis, a competitor and, ironically, the contractor's own nephew.

Begun in 1848, construction of the lighthouse was delayed by funding shortages and foul weather for almost four years. It was finally completed in 1852 by a crew working under the direction of a U.S. Army officer, Lieutenant George Meade. Like I. W. P. Lewis, Meade was an engineer and a child of the new, iron-willed machine age. Meade would later oversee construction of numerous other lighthouses, including those at Sand Key, completed in 1853, and Sombrero Key, completed in 1856. As General Meade—some years later—he would find a ray of light in a moment of darkness for his nation by leading the Union forces to victory at Gettysburg.

The Carysfort Reef Light was automated in 1958, but for more than a century a keeper and several assistants were on duty there at all times. Periodically, a tender brought supplies from Key West, and fresh water was kept in a 3,500-gallon tank and several 600-gallon auxiliary tanks. Keepers and assistants remained at the station for months at a stretch. The last keeper and crew left the station soon after the light was automated in 1858, and today, the old lighthouse is a lonely place indeed.

TO SEE THE LIGHT: The tower is distantly visible from Route 905 on Key Largo. To see it up close you must charter a boat; keep in mind, though, that visitors are not allowed on the structure. The lighthouse is now part of John Pennekamp Coral Reef State Park; call (305) 451–1202.

Location: Off Key Largo

Established: 1852

Tower height: 110 feet

Elevation of the focal plane: 100 feet

Optic: Modern (solar powered)

Status: Active

Characteristic: Flashes three times every 60 seconds

Range: 15 miles

Position: 25° 13' 18
         80° 12' 42

Note: Experimental iron-skeleton tower

ALLIGATOR REEF LIGHT

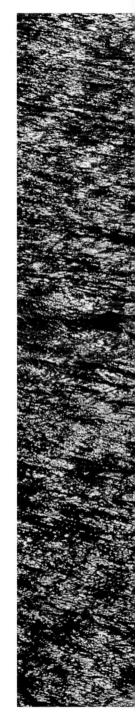

Affectionately known as "Old Gator," the Alligator Reef Light is as tough as a reptile. Built during the early 1870s on a wave-swept shoal off Matecumbe Key, the 136-foot iron-skeleton tower has withstood dozens of major hurricanes. Even the 1935 Labor Day super storm that slammed the tower with a 20-foot wall of water could not topple it.

Despite its playful moniker, neither Old Gator nor the ship-killing reef on which it stands is named for the American alligator. Instead, the names honor the U.S. Navy schooner USS *Alligator*, sunk here in 1822. Over the years countless vessels have followed the *Alligator* to their doom on the reef's jagged coral. To stop—or at least slow—the losses, the U.S. Lighthouse Board launched construction of a light tower here in 1870. Ironically, the project headquarters and workers' barracks were on nearby Indian Key, which was inhabited by wreckers who made their livings salvaging vessels caught by the reef.

Blows from a two-thousand-pound hammer drove 12-inch iron pilings 10 feet into the coral to support the tower. Iron discs helped anchor the pilings to the coral. Completed in 1873 at the then phenomenal cost of $185,000, Old Gator still stands tall. Its hefty first-order Fresnel lens has been replaced by a solar-powered modern optic, but its flashing beacon is no less effective.

TO SEE THE LIGHT: Driving the unique 126-mile Overseas Highway is a bit like motoring across the open ocean. Look to the southeast anywhere from Mile Marker 80, near the north end of Lower Matecumbe Key, to Mile Marker 77 to see the venerable Alligator Reef Light. To view or photograph the lighthouse at leisure, turn off the road at Mile Marker 79.

Location: Off Lower Matecumbe Key

Established: 1873

Tower height: 136 feet

Elevation of the focal plane: 136 feet

Optic: Modern (solar powered)

Status: Active

Characteristic: Flashes four times every 60 seconds

Range: 16 miles

Position: 24° 51' 06
80° 37' 06

Note: Most expensive lighthouse to construct in Florida

Although scheduled for construction in 1854, storms and funding shortages delayed completion of the Sombrero Key Lighthouse until 1858. Army engineer George Meade saw the project through to its end. The tower he and his work crews built here cost the government $150,000, a considerable fortune at the time, but the structure proved well worth its hefty price, standing up to gales and hurricanes for more than 140 years.

Meade placed the 160-foot tower atop galvanized steel pilings, an innovation that may account for the lighthouse's extraordinary longevity. Meade knew the reef rose out of the sea at low tide so that the foundation would be alternately bathed in salt water and exposed to the air every twelve hours. This would bring about a rapid deterioration of the iron pilings and they would eventually fail, causing the tower to collapse under its own weight. However, he believed the galvanized steel would resist the corrosive effects of the salt water. For added support, he had the pilings hammered through metal discs that helped anchor them securely to the underlying coral. History has proven the value of Meade's engineering skills—to the Union Army at Gettysburg and to the mariners whose lives it saved. The station's original first-order Fresnel lens, which cost $20,000, produced a fixed, white light visible up to 15 miles away. In 1931 the lens was fitted with revolving opaque screens that made the light appear to flash. In 1984 a modern optic powered by solar cells replaced the huge Fresnel lens.

TO SEE THE LIGHT: You can view the lighthouse from Sombrero Beach State Park near the town of Marathon on Vaca Key. The station's old first-order lens is on display in Key West. Contact the Key West Lighthouse Museum, 938 Whitehead Street, Key West, 33040; call (305) 294–0012.

Location: Near Marathon

Established: 1858

Tower height: 160 feet

Elevation of the focal plane: 142 feet

Optic: Modern (solar powered)

Status: Active

Characteristic: Flashes five times every 20 seconds (red sector)

Range: 15 miles

Position: 24° 37' 36
81° 06' 36

Note: Designed and built by George Meade

AMERICAN SHOAL LIGHT

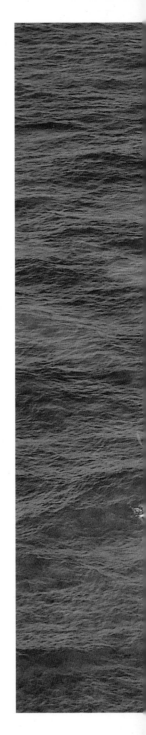

Location: Off
Sugarloaf Key

Established: 1880

Tower height: 109 feet

Elevation of the focal
plane: 109 feet

Optic: Modern
(solar powered)

Status: Active

Characteristic: Flashes
three times every
15 seconds

Range: 10 miles

Position: 24° 31' 30
81° 31' 12

Note: Near-twin of Fowey
Rocks Light

This killer reef, located about 20 miles northeast of Key West, has torn open the hulls of so many ships that the exact number will never be known. Early attempts to stop the carnage included placing daymarks on nearby keys and erecting a tall, unlighted piling atop the shoal. But vessels caught in the tricky currents near the shoal often saw these markers too late, and at night, of course, they were of no use at all. Finally, in 1878, Congress appropriated $75,000 to place a lighthouse directly over the shoal.

Fabricated in a New Jersey shipyard, the 109-foot tower was shipped nearly 1,500 miles south and installed atop a massive underwater platform. The final cost of the station, including the tower; the octagonal keeper's dwelling resting on a platform about 40 feet above the water; and the first-order Fresnel lens in the lantern room at the top came to $125,000, nearly twice the original estimate. A reluctant Congress finally coughed up the necessary additional funds, and the station's lamps shone out for the first time on July 15, 1880.

The Coast Guard automated the light in 1963, removing not just the station's keepers but also its rotating, clamshell Fresnel lens. The modern optic currently in place is powered by batteries recharged by solar cells.

TO SEE THE LIGHT: Near Overseas Highway Mile Marker 17 on Sugarloaf Key, turn left on Sugarloaf Boulevard (Route 939), then right on Route 939A. The lighthouse can be seen in the ocean to the southeast of a bridge across a small inlet.

SAND KEY LIGHT

In 1827 the government established a light station on Sand Key, a soggy and nearly barren island a few miles from Key West. Its 65-foot brick tower held an array of whale-oil lamps and reflectors, and for nearly twenty years it guided ships through the safe channels south of the Keys. Then, in October 1846, a devastating hurricane swept away the station and even the island on which it had stood. Tragically, keeper Joshua Appleby and several station visitors were killed by the storm.

After the Sand Key station and its keeper drowned, a lightship marked the key until a new lighthouse could be built. Completed in 1853, the new iron-skeleton tower rose 120 feet above what was now open water. Perhaps with the 1846 disaster in mind, its designers gave the tower a solid footing of twelve hefty steel pilings and heavily braced legs sloping inward toward the lantern. Fitted with a first-order Fresnel lens, its flashing light could warn mariners up to 20 miles away. The grand old Fresnel was removed when the station was automated in 1941 just before the United States entered World War II. Nearly destroyed in 1989 by a fire that started in the abandoned keeper's dwelling, the lighthouse has been restored at a cost of $500,000.

TO SEE THE LIGHT: The lighthouse and its beacon can be seen distantly from nearby Key West; it can be seen up close only from the water or air. For information on boat charters from Key West or flying services offering flights to Sand Key, contact the Key West Chamber of Commerce, 402 Wall Street, Key West, 33040; call (800) 527–8539.

Location: Near Key West

Established: 1827

Tower height: 120 feet

Elevation of the focal plane: 109 feet

Optic: Modern (solar powered)

Status: Active

Characteristic: Flashes twice every 15 seconds (red sector)

Range: 14 miles

Position: 24° 27' 14 81° 52' 39

Note: Hurricane swept away earlier lighthouse and its keeper

KEY WEST LIGHTHOUSE

U ntil the United States took possession of Florida from the Spanish in 1821, Key West had been home port to a large fleet of buccaneers. The pirates had preyed on the lucrative shipping that linked South America to Europe and New Orleans. U.S. Navy frigates soon sent the pirates packing, but even then the Keys remained a stronghold of maritime predators. Only now, instead of privateers, they called themselves salvagers or, more commonly, "wreckers." Rather than take the riches they sought with cannon and cutlass, the wreckers let the deadly Florida reefs do their dirty work for them. Whenever a ship came to grief on the shoals, the wreckers swooped down on the hapless vessel to plunder its cargo.

To reduce this wanton, semilegal thievery and make the Keys safer for navigation, the U.S. government began to mark the low, sandy islands and nearby reefs with lighthouses. The first was built in 1825 on Whitehead Point near the bustling harbor of Key West, which attracted vast quantities of commerce, much of it salvaged from shipwrecks in the Keys. A 65-foot brick tower, the harbor lighthouse was destroyed by the same mighty 1846 hurricane that swallowed up Sand Key and devastated much of Key West.

By 1847 a new Key West Lighthouse had been built on a more secure site farther from the water. A third-order Fresnel lens placed in the lantern in 1872 improved the range of the beacon. So, too, did the 20 feet added to the height of the tower in 1892.

The Key West Light was decommissioned in 1969. Presently, the lighthouse serves as one of many attractions in this sunny, water-besieged tourist Mecca.

TO SEE THE LIGHT: The lighthouse and the Key West Lighthouse Museum (housed in the station's old keeper's bungalow) are located at the intersection of Truman Avenue (U.S. Highway 1) and Whitehead Street. Among the wide array of fascinating museum exhibits is a fourth-order Fresnel bull's-eye lens. Contact the Key West Lighthouse Museum, 938 Whitehead Street, Key West, 33040; call (305) 294–0012. For additional information and travel assistance call the Key West Chamber of Commerce at (800) 527–8539.

Location: Key West

Established: 1825

Tower height: 86 feet

Elevation of the focal plane: 91 feet

Optic: Fresnel lens (third order) removed

Status: Deactivated in 1969

Note: Former stronghold of pirates

Photo courtesy of Lighthouse Digest Magazine

REBECCA SHOAL LIGHTHOUSE

Gales and hurricanes have swept through the passage between Key West and the Dry Tortugas so frequently that U.S. maritime officials found it almost impossible to establish a light station here. Work began on the Rebecca Shoal Lighthouse in 1854, but the tower was blown apart by a storm before it could be placed in service. The same thing happened several times over the next three decades and, remarkably, the project was not completed until 1886, more than thirty years after it began.

Although building the lighthouse had tested the patience of an entire generation of engineers and work crews, it was not a complex structure. Consisting of a two-story wooden dwelling with a small lantern on its roof, it stood on a platform held above the water by braced steel legs anchored securely to the sea bottom by screw piles. Similar to cottage style lighthouses more commonly seen in protected waters such as the Chesapeake Bay, the Rebecca Shoal Lighthouse proved more durable than might have been expected. It resisted the battering of wind and water for more than sixty-five years, but by the early 1950s it had begun to fall apart.

In 1953 the ramshackle lighthouse was torn down. Although the old lighthouse is gone, the beacon that replaced it remains in place. Its modest flashing light can be seen from about 9 miles away.

TO SEE THE LIGHT: Most "Lost Lighthouses" survive only in books like this one or in the memories of those lucky enough to have seen them, but the Rebecca Shoal Lighthouse has an operating beacon as a memorial. Clearly marked on navigational charts—at 24° 34' 42, 82° 35' 06—the existing Rebecca Shoal Lighthouse can be seen from tour boats making the passage from Key West to Dry Tortugas National Park. For more information on available transportation and the park itself, call (305) 242–7700.

The early twentieth-century photograph at left shows Rebecca Shoal Lighthouse standing atop its spidery legs and piles. Today nothing remains of this sturcture, and a small skeleton tower now does the work of warning mariners away from the shoal.

Location: Between Key West and Garden Key

Established: 1886

Tower height: 70 feet

Elevation of the focal plane: 66 feet

Optic: Fresnel lens (fourth order) removed

Status: Deactivated and destroyed in 1953

Note: Took more than 30 years to complete

GARDEN KEY LIGHTHOUSE

About 120 miles west of the Florida peninsula, a scatter of small islands and reefs known as the Dry Tortugas rise out of the Gulf of Mexico. Unpredictable currents combine with a jumble of ship-killing shoals to make this one of the most dangerous places in all the world's oceans. To warn mariners the U.S. government established a light station on Garden Key in 1826, but not without considerable difficulty. Dramatizing the need for the light, one of the ships carrying materials for the 70-foot brick tower wrecked on the very shoals the light was intended to guard.

By 1846 the tower's lantern barely peaked above Fort Jefferson, an impressive structure with walls 50 feet high and 8 feet thick, and containing more than forty million bricks. Fort Jefferson's 450 smooth-bore cannons were capable of pummeling an entire enemy fleet but were never once fired in anger. Instead, the fort served as a prison, its most notable inmate being Maryland physician Samuel Mudd, thrown into a stinking cell for having—innocently enough—set the broken leg of Lincoln assassin John Wilkes Booth. President Grant pardoned Dr. Mudd in 1869 for his humanitarian efforts during a yellow-fever epidemic.

A hurricane ruined the original Garden Key Light in 1873. Its replacement, completed three years later, consisted of a 37-foot cast-iron tower positioned atop the walls of the fort. Its fourth-order Fresnel lens, illuminated by kerosene lamps, gave the beacon a range of approximately 16 miles. The light was decommissioned in 1912.

TO SEE THE LIGHT: Garden Key and its lighthouse are part of Dry Tortugas National Park, which encompasses nearly 65,000 acres of coral reef and churning surf but only forty acres of dry land. Attractions include historic Fort Jefferson and a 100-square-mile naturalist's paradise, where ocean mammals, sharks, fish, and seabirds of every variety abound. Charter boats, ferries, and scheduled seaplane service are available from Key West. Contact the Key West Chamber of Commerce, 402 Wall Street, Key West, 33040; call (800) 527–8539. Additional information is available from Dry Tortugas National Park, P.O. Box 6208, Key West, 33041; call (305) 242–7700.

Location: Dry Tortugas

Established: 1826

Tower height: 37 feet

Optic: Fresnel lens
(fourth order) removed

Status: Deactivated
in 1912

Note: Dr. Samuel Mudd
imprisoned here

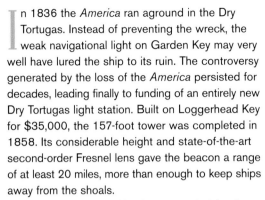

DRY TORTUGAS LIGHT

I n 1836 the *America* ran aground in the Dry Tortugas. Instead of preventing the wreck, the weak navigational light on Garden Key may very well have lured the ship to its ruin. The controversy generated by the loss of the *America* persisted for decades, leading finally to funding of an entirely new Dry Tortugas light station. Built on Loggerhead Key for $35,000, the 157-foot tower was completed in 1858. Its considerable height and state-of-the-art second-order Fresnel lens gave the beacon a range of at least 20 miles, more than enough to keep ships away from the shoals.

Severely damaged by the same 1873 hurricane that destroyed the lighthouse on neighboring Garden Key, the tower was at first thought to be a complete loss. Masons sent to do emergency repairs did their work so well that the tower still stands, survivor of at least a dozen additional major hurricanes.

Because of its remote location, in 1925 the station was outfitted with an automatic acetylene lamp to replace its full-time crew. A modern optic superseded the original clamshell Fresnel lens in 1986; it displays a flashing white light seen from up to 20 miles.

TO SEE THE LIGHT: Loggerhead Key and its lighthouse are located within the 65,000-acre Dry Tortugas National Park. For information on charter boats, ferries, and seaplanes providing access to the park, contact the Key West Chamber of Commerce, 402 Wall Street, Key West, 33040; call (800) 527–8539. Information is also available from Dry Tortugas National Park, P.O. Box 6208, Key West, 33041; call (305) 242–7700.

Location: Loggerhead Key

Established: 1858

Tower height: 157 feet

Elevation of the focal
plane: 151 feet

Optic: Modern
(solar powered)

Status: Active

Characteristic: Flashes
white every 20 seconds

Range: 20 miles

Position: 24° 38' 00
82° 55' 12

Note: Last Keys light
seen by ships entering
the Gulf of Mexico

CHAPTER THREE:
SANIBEL TO CEDAR KEY

With its pristine beaches, mangrove swamps, and estuaries teeming with fish, the west coast of the Florida peninsula is a natural wonderland as well as a magnet for sun-loving tourists. Its beauty is renowned, but most who come here to enjoy the scenery are unaware of the region's tumultuous history. Explorers were so fearful of these shores that this part of Florida remained a blank spot on the map for centuries. Later it became a lair of pirates and then a battleground for forces of the Blue and Gray during the Civil War. Historians and travel writers believe they have reason for referring to this area as the "Wild West of Florida," but, no doubt, over the years mariners have coined sterner expressions to describe it.

The region's southern extremity is dominated by the swampy netherworld of the Everglades. There are no major navigational lights here for the very good reason that ships avoid these waters at all cost. Any vessel swept by storms into the shallow Florida Bay north of the Keys is likely never to be seen again.

Mariners seeking a bright light to help them find shelter from storms must look well to the north of the Everglades mangroves to Charlotte Harbor and Sanibel Island, where a nautical light has called to them for more than a century. So dangerous are the waters near Sanibel that, during the 1880s, a tender bringing materials to build the lighthouse struck a shoal and sunk. Despite this disaster, the lighthouse was eventually completed, and many ships have been saved by its beacon.

Also marking the approaches to Charlotte Harbor are the Port Boca Grande and Gasparilla Island Lights. These beacons line up one behind the other to help vessels stay on course and keep within the narrow safe channel. Both stations are located on Gasparilla Island, said to be named for Gaspar, a notorious buccaneer. As its name suggests, the island was once infested by pirates who used it as a base for raids on shipping and small Florida coastal communities.

Any pirates who sailed into Tampa Bay had to take their chances with its tricky currents and dangerous shoals. After 1848, by which time the U.S. Navy had long since driven pirates out of the Gulf of Mexico, vessels plying these waters could depend on Egmont Key Light for guidance. The island and its lighthouse have a fascinating past that sheds a revealing light on the history of Florida's entire Gulf Coast.

Hernando DeSoto may have been the first European to set foot on the small, sandy island known today as Egmont Key. Some believe that DeSoto pitched camp on the island in 1539 before launching his famous exploration of the North American interior—a trek that would take him all the way to the Mississippi River. But it was the British who gave the key its unusual name, almost two centuries later, when a royal survey team charted the Gulf Coast. The name honors the Earl of Egmont, who was at that time Lord of the Admiralty. One might wonder why the earl rated so small an honor—why, for instance, his surveyors had not attached his name to the impressive bay behind the little island or to the vast peninsula beyond. The answer, of course, is that the Spanish had long ago given names to those particular natural features: They were called Tampa Bay and Florida.

After Florida became part of the United States in 1821, Tampa Bay emerged as an important trading center, and its commercial vitality steadily increased. By the 1830s Florida settlers were asking the federal government to mark the bay with a lighthouse, but no action was taken for nearly two decades. A lighthouse was finally built on Egmont Key in 1848 by contractor Francis Gibbons for $10,000. Despite a five-month delay due to a lack of bricks—none could be found for sale along the entire coast of western Florida—the contractor had the tower and a small keeper's dwelling standing in just over half a year. Having earned a reputation at Egmont Key for solid workmanship, Gibbons was later hired to build the first lighthouses on the coasts of California, Oregon, and Washington State.

The same year Gibbons completed its lighthouse, Egmont Key was visited by an army surveyor with a name now known to every American: Robert E. Lee. Although Lee thought the strategically located island an ideal location for a stone fort, none was ever built there. However, the brick walls of the new light tower at the north end of the island soon earned a reputation for being as strong as a fortress.

The storms kept coming, year after year, and while their winds never quite managed to topple the tower, flooding tides eventually undermined it. In 1858 the original Gibbons lighthouse had to be torn down and rebuilt. Masons reinforced the new 87-foot masonry tower with walls more than 3 feet thick. Those stout, brick walls have since stood up to more than 140 years of hurricanes and gales. Located at the north end of the island, the structure still stands, and its automated light remains active.

SANIBEL ISLAND LIGHT

D uring the 1920s automaker Henry Ford and his old friend Thomas Edison came to Florida's Fort Myers each year to escape the long northern winter. The two men shared an occasional ferry outing to lush Sanibel Island, located a few miles off the mainland. No doubt, when they made the crossing during the evening, their eyes caught the flash of the Sanibel Island Light on Point Ybel. Ironically, the light they saw was not produced by one of Mr. Edison's lightbulbs. Instead, it came from a kerosene lamp. (Somewhat later the station would employ an acetylene lamp.) The lighthouse did not receive an electric lamp until 1962, making it one of the last light stations in America to be electrified.

Time—and what some like to call progress—often move slowly on beautiful Sanibel. The lighthouse itself was a very long time coming. By 1833 early island settlers and local fishermen were already petitioning Congress for a light. Their pleas fell on deaf ears until the 1850s, when the newly formed U.S. Lighthouse Board recommended that a light station be placed here. Still nothing was done, and Congress appropriated no money for the project until 1883, a full half century after the first petitions were submitted.

With $50,000 in federal money available for the project, a supply ship carrying iron for the station's tower set sail from New Jersey bound for Sanibel. Only a few miles short of the island, it struck a shoal and sank. Salvagers from Key West managed to pull most of the materials off the sandy sea bottom, and at long last construction of the tower got underway. The station's lamps were officially lit on August 20, 1884.

An iron skeleton—style structure, designed to withstand hurricane winds, the tower stands on four legs braced by steel girds and tie bars. A central metal-walled cylinder provides access to the lantern via a winding staircase of 127 steps. Soaring 100 feet above the low, sandy point, the lantern room once housed a third-order Fresnel lens that displayed a flashing white beacon. The light guided ships past Point Ybel and into the nearby deep-water port of Punta Rassa. The old French-made glass lens was replaced with a modern plastic lens some years ago when the station was automated, and the light remains active to this day.

The tower is listed on the National Register of Historic Places. So, too, are the adjacent tropical-style keeper's cottages. Built on piles, the cottages have steeply sloped pyramidal roofs and wide, wraparound verandas.

Location: Sanibel Island

Established: 1884

Tower height: 102 feet

Elevation of the focal plane: 98 feet

Optic: Modern optic

Status: Active

Characteristic: Flashes twice every 6 seconds

Range: 13 miles

Position: 26° 27' 11
82° 00' 51

Note: Said to be haunted

TO SEE THE LIGHT: This lighthouse is not open to the public, but visitors are welcome to walk the grounds and photograph the tower. From Fort Myers follow the Sanibel Causeway, Highway 867, and Lighthouse Road to the J.N. "Ding" Darling National Wildlife Refuge. The refuge's visitor center is located on One Wildlife Drive, just off San-Cap Road. The original Sanibel Island third-order lens is now on display at the Sanibel Historical Museum at 850 Dunlop Road, Sanibel, 33957; call (941) 472–4648.

Bob and Sandra Shanklin,
The Lighthouse People

GASPARILLA ISLAND LIGHT

I n 1932, as one of many steps taken to boost a Florida economy hard-pressed by the Great Depression, a range-light system was established on Gasparilla Island. It was intended to guide freighters carrying Florida phosphates to chemical plants along the Mississippi and, thus, provide jobs for chemical workers and seamen.

The lower front-range light was already in place atop the Port Boca Grande tower located down near the Gasparilla Island beaches. Rather than build an all-new rear-range tower, maritime officials decided to use an existing structure that had served since 1891 in faraway Delaware. The 105-foot steel-skeleton Delaware Breakwater tower was taken apart piece by piece and shipped to Florida where it was reassembled.

Like other range-light systems, this one guided vessels with a pair of lights. If the beacons appear vertically aligned, an approaching helmsmen can be sure they are in a safe channel.

TO SEE THE LIGHT: To reach Gasparilla Island from U.S. Highway 41, follow Routes 776 and 771 to Placida, then follow signs to the Boca Grande Causeway and toll bridge leading to Gasparilla Island. The lighthouse is located within Gasparilla Island State Park; call (941) 964–0375.

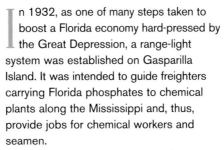

Location: Gasparilla Island

Established: 1932

Tower height: 105 feet

Elevation of the focal plane: 105 feet

Optic: Modern

Status: Active

Characteristic: Flashes every 6 seconds

Range: 12 miles

Position: 26° 44' 31
82° 15' 48

Note: This tower originally stood in Delaware

PORT BOCA GRANDE LIGHT

B uilt in 1890 on Gasparilla Island, the Port Boca Grande beacon lights the southern stretches of the Florida coast and, some say, marks the grave of a headless Spanish princess. The island is named for José Gaspar, a bloodthirsty pirate with a lusty appetite for gold, silver, and women. Gaspar's raids on merchant ships netted him female prisoners, some of whom he kept on Gasparilla, which he called "Cautiva," meaning "captive woman."

According to legend, one of Gaspar's captives, a Spanish princess named Josefa, turned the tables on the pirate by imprisoning his heart. Gaspar was so stricken with the lady that he begged her to marry him. However, the proud Josefa answered his marriage plea with a curse and spat in his eye. In a fit of rage, the pirate drew his saber and beheaded her. Overwhelmed with remorse, Gaspar buried Josefa's body on the beach where he had murdered her. To remind him of his love for the princess, he kept her head in a jar on his ship. It is said that Josefa's decapitated ghost still walks the island in search of its missing head.

If Josefa's body was ever buried on Gasparilla Island, it likely washed away in the surf many years ago. The beaches here are constantly eroding, a process that threatens every structure on the island including the Port Boca Grande Light. Completed in 1890 at a cost of $35,000, the square, wooden structure was built on piles to protect it from the tides. The lighthouse held its own for nearly a century, but by 1970 seawater was washing away the sand around its supports. Construction of a 265-foot granite jetty helped saved the historic building. So, too, did the Gasparilla Island Conservation Association, which raised funds to restore the lighthouse after the Coast Guard abandoned it in 1967. The station was relit and returned to service in 1986.

TO SEE THE LIGHT: The lighthouse is located on Gulf Boulevard at the far southern tip of the island. From Placida follow signs to the Boca Grande Causeway and toll bridge leading to Gasparilla Island. Meticulously restored during the 1980s, the old lighthouse was recently opened as a museum. Contact the Boca Grande Lighthouse Museum, P.O. Box 637, Boca Grande, 33921; call (941) 964–0060.

Location: Gasparilla Island

Established: 1890

Tower height: 30 feet

Elevation of the focal plane: 41 feet

Optic: Drum lens

Status: Active

Characteristic: Occulting every 4 seconds

Range: 12 miles

Position: 26° 43' 02 82° 15' 39

Note: Wide wraparound veranda adds grace and architectural interest

EGMONT KEY LIGHT

ernando DeSoto may have been the first European to set foot on the small, sandy island known today as Egmont Key. Some believe that DeSoto pitched camp on he island in 1539, before launching his famous exploration of the American interior—a trek that would take him all the way to the Mississippi River. But it was the British who gave the key its unusual name, almost two centuries later, when a royal survey team charted the Gulf Coast. The name honors the Earl of Egmont, who was at that time Lord of the Admiralty. One might wonder why the earl rated so small an honor— why, for instance, his surveyors did not attach his name to the impressive bay behind the island to the vast peninsula beyond. The answer, of course, is that the Spanish had long before given names to those natural features. They are called Tampa Bay and Florida.

After Florida became part of the United States in 1821, the commercial and navigational importance the Gulf Coast steadily increased.

In 1848 contractor Francis Gibbons completed a lighthouse on Egmont Key to serve the rapidly developing Tampa Bay area. Gibbons would later build the first lighthouses on the coasts of California, Oregon, and Washington State, many of which still stand. The lighthouse he built for $10,000 on Egmont Key, a small island named for an eighteenth-century British admiral, lasted only ten years, however. Repeatedly pounded by hurricanes so powerful they frightened one keeper into early retirement, it had to be torn down and rebuilt in 1858.

Masons reinforced the new 87-foot masonry tower with brick walls more than 3 feet thick. These stout walls have stood up to near one and a half centuries of hurricanes and gales. Located at the north end of Egmont Key, the structure still stands. Unfortunately, its lantern has been removed, so this tower is not as attractive as some. Even so, the Egmont Key Light remains a hard-working aid to navigation, and its light continues to guide vessels in and out of Tampa Bay.

TO SEE THE LIGHT: Egmont Key and its lighthouse are accessible only by boat, but you can see and enjoy the signal from nearby Fort De Soto State Park. To reach the park follow Routes 682 and 679 south from St. Petersburg. For more information call the Greater Tampa Chamber of Commerce at (813) 228–7777.

Location: Egmont Key near St. Petersburg

Established: 1848

Tower height: 87 feet

Elevation of the focal plane: 85 feet

Optic: Modern

Status: Active

Characteristic: Flashes every 15 seconds

Range: 24 miles

Position: 27° 36' 03
82° 45' 38

Note: Hurricanes drove off the keeper

ANCLOTE KEY LIGHT

Location: Anclote Key

Established: 1887

Tower height: 102 feet

Elevation of the focal plane: 110 feet

Optic: Modern

Status: Private aid to navigation

Characteristic: Flashes four times every 30 seconds

Range: 19 miles

Position: 28° 10' 02 82° 50' 44

Note: Endangered lighthouse now restored and reactivated

Anclote Key, a long, thin Gulf island just to the west of Tarpon Springs, has always been popular with insects. People, on the other hand, often find the place less inviting. For many years the keepers of the Anclote Key Light were the island's only human inhabitants and, constantly under assault by clouds of hungry mosquitoes, even they were not always glad to be there.

For a brief period in 1682, however, Anclote Key was one of the busiest spots in Florida. Early that year an entire fleet of pirate ships anchored there, and more than 400 buccaneers went ashore to sharpen their cutlasses and ready themselves for raids along the nearby coast. Using the island as a base, this lawless armada attacked and devastated dozens of small, defenseless mainland settlements. Then, a few months after they had arrived, the pirates moved on to overwhelm the Spanish fort at San Marcos.

More than two centuries would pass before the island was invaded again, this time by construction workers hired in 1887 to build the Anclote Key Light. Like the earlier invasion, this one would be brief. Prefabricated in a northern shipyard, the 102-foot, steel-skeleton tower was bolted together quickly. Begun in June, the station was completed and ready for service within two months. Keeper James Gardner lit the kerosene lamps inside the third-order Fresnel lens on September 15, 1887. Displaying four red flashes every thirty seconds, the beacon could be distinguished easily from that of the white light on nearby Egmont Key.

The Anclote Key keepers and their families, who often lived with them on the island, suffered through the same powerful storms and flood tides that plagued other Gulf Coast light stations. But the keepers' worst—and certainly most annoying—problem was island's prodigious population of mosquitoes. Drainage canals, dug by Depression-era Works Progress Administration workers hoping to control the droning pests, did little to keep them down. No doubt, it was with a sense of relief that the last keepers left the island when the Coast Guard discontinued the light in 1952.

Although abandoned nearly half a century ago, the old tower still stands. The dwelling and other station buildings, however, were long ago removed. The tower might have been lost as well had not the Gulf Islands Alliance and other preservation-minded groups stepped in to save it. Federal, state, and private funds were pledged to the preservation effort, and, happily, the lighthouse has been both restored and relit. On September 13, 2003, the station's beacon was ceremoniously returned to service as a private aid to navigation. Located in the Anclote Key Preserve State Park, the lighthouse is owned by the State of Florida.

TO SEE THE LIGHT: Anclote Key is about 3 miles off Tarpon Springs and can be reached only by boat. Call (727) 944–4468 for information on cruises that pass near the island and its historic lighthouse. Call (727) 469–5918 for information on Anclote Key Preserve State Park. For more information on the lighthouse and the effort to save it, call the Gulf Islands Alliance at (813) 968–5640.

CEDAR KEYS LIGHTHOUSE

U sed in the manufacture of pencils, Cedar Keys hardwood attracted such an endless parade of lumber ships that the government established a light station here in 1854. Built under the watchful eye of U.S. Army engineer George Meade, the lighthouse stands on Seahorse Key, about 3 miles southwest of Cedar Key, the largest island in the chain. Unlike the iron-skeleton towers

he built in south Florida, Meade gave this lighthouse a one-story brick dwelling and placed a small tower on its roof. The entire project cost $12,000, little more than 10 percent of the bill Meade handed Congress for some of his other towers.

Although only 28 feet high, the Cedar Keys Lighthouse stands on a hill, placing the focal plane of its beacon some 75 feet above the water. The elevation helped make its fixed white light visible from more than 12 miles away.

During the last years of the nineteenth century, the economy of the Cedar Key area fell on hard times, and the Cedar Keys Lighthouse was permanently darkened in 1915. Seahorse Key is now part of the Cedar Keys National Wildlife Refuge. The University of Florida uses the old lighthouse as a marine laboratory.

TO SEE THE LIGHT: Located in an environmentally sensitive wildlife refuge, Seahorse Key is closed to the public but can be seen from the water. For excursions contact the Cedar Key Chamber of Commerce, P.O. Box 610, Cedar Key, 32625; call (352) 543–5600. Known for its great fishing and seafood, the Cedar Key area can be reached from U.S. Highway 19 or Interstate 75 via Route 24 south.

Location: Seahorse Key

Established: 1854

Tower height: 28 feet

Elevation of the focal plane: 75 feet

Optic: Fresnel lens (fourth order) removed

Status: Deactivated in 1915

Note: Now serves as a marine laboratory

Its beacon inactive since 1965, Cedar Keys Lighthouse now lights the way for marine scientists rather than ships.
Bob and Sandra Shanklin, The Lighthouse People

CHAPTER FOUR:
ST. MARKS TO PENSACOLA

overing 582,100 square miles in a blanket of warm tropical water averaging a mile in depth, the Gulf of Mexico is enclosed on three and almost four sides by land. Often, however, the shores of the Gulf are not dry land in the usual sense. The swamps, marshes, and barrier islands that line its shores seem undecided as to whether they belong to the sea or the land. In fact they may change status each time a major hurricane passes through and exposed sandbars and low islands are converted to shoals lurking just beneath the surface. This vacillating quality of the Gulf Coast makes it an extraordinarily dangerous place for ships and seamen.

As is the case elsewhere along the Gulf, the Florida panhandle confronts navigators with an ever-changing shoreline and a bewildering maze of shoals and other natural obstacles. As currents shape and reshape the border between land and water, subsurface sandbanks and entire islands migrate from place to place. Waters that are safe one week may be deadly the next.

Storms compound mariners' problems. The Gulf is known as "hurricane alley" for good reason: More than half the hurricanes that spin northward out of the Caribbean strike land at some point along its coast. Major hurricanes—those described by the National Weather Service as "category four or five"—may strike with winds up to 200 miles per hour and a force equal to several nuclear blasts. Given sufficient warning, sailors and their ships will run for open water and ride out the storm at sea—better that than be caught in the shoal-strewn, hull-grinding narrows near the land. Although lighthouses and other structures cannot get out of the way, most people on shore will also choose to make a run for it and seek safety somewhere inland.

Nowadays, vulnerable coastal areas are usually evacuated well before a hurricane hits, but in the old days these fierce storms struck with little or no warning. During the nineteenth century hurricanes swept away entire communities or damaged them so severely that they never fully recovered. In 1841 a hurricane so thoroughly blasted the thriving port of St. Joseph that its surviving residents fled the area never to return. Miraculously, the four-year-old St. Joseph Lighthouse remained standing after the storm, but with no port left to serve, it was soon abandoned.

The Gulf has seen few storms as ferocious as the one that swept over the panhandle in 1873, bringing with it a wall of water that eradicated nearly every structure that stood in its way. Not surprisingly, the lighthouses that stood in the storm's path were exposed to the worst of its fury. When the hurricane had passed, little remained but rubble of the once proud light stations at Cape San Blas and Cape St. George. The Dog Island Lighthouse had simply vanished along with the keeper and his family. Even the foundations of its tower and residence had been washed away.

The Dog Island Lighthouse was rebuilt but later abandoned after yet another hurricane carried away the island itself. The beacons at Cape San Blas and Cape St. George were likewise returned to service, but neither of the rebuilt towers would stand for long. The new Cape St. George Lighthouse lasted less than a year before a gale knocked it over, while the new tower at Cape San Blas was soon cut down by erosion. The government had no choice but to restore these important navigational stations, which over the years have been rebuilt or relocated repeatedly. Obviously, keeping the shores of the panhandle lit has tried the patience of federal maritime officials, but fortunately for mariners and for those of us who love history and lighthouses, they have shown determination.

ST. MARKS LIGHT

S ome say early Spanish explorers placed a light near the mouth of the St. Marks River to help their supply ships find them. If this were true, then it might be argued that North America's first lighthouse was built in Florida during 1500s, rather than at Boston in 1716. But if there ever was a Spanish light at St. Marks, it was long gone by the time U.S. authorities took charge of the area following the acquisition of Florida in 1821. Maritime officials could clearly see, however, that the strategic river mouth needed a navigational light, and Congress soon provided funds for one.

The early history of the St. Marks Light station was less than stellar. The workmanship of the first tower built there in 1831 proved so shoddy that officials ordered it torn down lest it fall of its own accord. Rebuilt that same year, it lasted only until 1840, when erosion forced relocation of the station. A third St. Marks tower was blown up by Confederate raiders during the Civil War.

The conical tower seen there today dates from 1867. Built atop a 12-foot-deep limestone foundation, its 4-foot-thick walls rise more than 73 feet into the Florida sky. Its automated light shines about 8 miles out to sea.

TO SEE THE LIGHT: The St. Marks Light is located in a pristine coastal game refuge. Although the station is closed to the public, visitors are welcome to walk the grounds and enjoy the unmatched scenery. Follow Route 363 from Tallahassee to the St. Marks National Wildlife Refuge, then County Road 59 to the lighthouse.

Location: St. Marks

Established: 1831

Tower height: 73 feet

Elevation of the focal plane: 82 feet

Optic: Modern

Status: Private aid to navigation

Characteristic: Occulting every 4 seconds

Range: 8 miles

Position: 30° 04' 18 84° 10' 48

Note: Earlier lighthouse blown up by Civil War raiders

CROOKED RIVER LIGHTHOUSE

O n September 18, 1873, a major hurricane struck the Florida panhandle, blasting the Dog Island Lighthouse, which had guided vessels into St. George Sound and along to Apalachicola since 1838. The storm swept away the entire station, and the U.S. Lighthouse Board wisely decided not to rebuild the exposed Dog Island Lighthouse. This left the area without a beacon for more than twenty years.

During the 1890s lumber freighters flocked to the Crooked River just north of Dog Island to take on loads of hardwood. To guide them a lighthouse was built near the mouth of the river, this time on the more stable ground of the mainland. Its designers took into account the special geology and weather condi-tions of the Gulf Coast. Its open, iron-skeleton design allows hurricane-force winds to pass through the tower without doing serious damage. The 115-foot tower has stood now for more than a century. Its flashing light continued to serve mariners until 1995 when the Coast Guard deactivated the station.

TO SEE THE LIGHT: You can see the lighthouse from U.S. Highway 98, about a mile west of Carrabelle. The station is closed to the public, but the tall red-and-white tower soaring toward the sky is an inspiring sight.

Location: Carrabelle

Established: 1895

Tower height: 115 feet

Elevation of the focal plane: 125 feet

Optic: Fresnel lens (fourth order) removed

Status: Deactivated in 1995

Note: Also known as the Carrabelle Light

DOG ISLAND LIGHTHOUSE

Winslow Lewis built the first tower on Dog Island, a shifting pile of sand near the entrance to St. George Bay. Completed in 1839, it was undermined by storm-driven tides just two years later. Lewis pulled down the ruined 50-foot brick tower and replaced it with a wooden structure. The mighty 1851 panhandle hurricane left only splinters of this second structure. A third Dog Island Lighthouse was burned by Union raiders during the Civil War, while the fourth and final one succumbed to a storm in 1873.

TO SEE THE LIGHT: The Dog Island Lighthouse vanished more than one and a quarter centuries ago, and so, cannot be visited. Even the island on which it stood has long since sunk beneath the Gulf of Mexico. However, a very similar lighthouse can be seen on St. George Island near Apalachicola. For information on access to this scenic barrier island and its lighthouse call the Apalachicola Chamber of Commerce at (850) 653–8219.

Location: Dog Island

Established: 1839

Tower height: 50 feet

Status: Destroyed in 1873

Note: Rebuilt several times

CAPE ST. GEORGE LIGHTHOUSE

L arge quantities of cotton once flowed into Apalachicola on its way to distant ports in New England and Europe. To guide freighters into Apalachicola Bay, the government established a light station on St. George Island in 1833. Well-known contractor Winslow Lewis built the 70-foot brick lighthouse for $9,500, fitting it with one of his own patented lamp-and-reflector systems. As was the case with many Lewis lighthouses, the St. George Island beacon proved far less than adequate, and its light reached only a few miles out to sea.

Bowled over by an 1851 hurricane that leveled several Florida light stations, the Cape St. George Lighthouse was rebuilt in 1852. Since then, it has successfully weathered dozens of major storms and even a Civil War cannonade by Confederates who tried but failed to destroy it. Seriously threatened by beach erosion, the Cape St. George tower is considered one of America's most endangered lighthouses. Over the years the erosion has undercut the tower, causing it to lean queasily out of plumb and threatening to dump it into the Gulf of Mexico. An innovative plan to straighten the tower and stabilize the surrounding sands appears to have succeeded, but the sea may yet claim its victim.

TO SEE THE LIGHT: St. George Island and its lighthouse can only be reached by boat. For more information on access to this scenic area, contact the Apalachicola Chamber of Commerce at (850) 653–8219. For more information on the continuing restoration effort or to lend a helping hand, write to the Cape St. George Lighthouse Society, P.O. Box 915, Apalachicola, 32329.

Location: St. George Island

Established: 1833

Tower height: 70 feet

Elevation of the focal plane: 70 feet

Optic: Fresnel lens (third order) removed

Status: Deactivated in 1994

Note: Leaning tower saved by innovative restoration effort

CAPE SAN BLAS LIGHTHOUSE

A few miles west of the Apalachicola River mouth, the Florida Panhandle juts out into the Gulf of Mexico. Here, sand and silt churned up by the swirling currents have formed an angular navigational obstacle called Cape San Blas. The same natural processes that created the cape also built up a series of dangerous shoals extended four to five miles out into the Gulf. Constantly shifting and frequently raked by powerful storms, these shoals are a mariner's nightmare. Keeping a light on the cape to warn ships has likewise proven a nightmare for goverment officials.

The Cape San Blas Lighthouse stood for only three years before the 1851 hurricane that destroyed the Dog Island Lighthouse knocked it down. Yellow fever delayed construction of a replacement. Masons finally laid the last bricks of the new tower in 1856, just in time to see it toppled by another hurricane. A third tower, completed in 1859, served for less than two years before Confederate forces snuffed out its lamps, removing the third-order Fresnel lens and setting fire to the tower. Renovated following the Civil War, the tower held out against repeated buffetings by gales and flood tides until 1882, when erosion cut the foundation away and it toppled into the Gulf.

A ship carrying materials needed to rebuild this hard-luck lighthouse sank off Sanibel Island; the new tower was not completed until 1885. This time, however, the U.S. Lighthouse Board wisely chose an iron-skeleton design capable of withstanding hurricane winds, and put the tower together in such a way that it can be taken apart and reassembled elsewhere whenever threatened by the Gulf's bulldozer-like tides. This approach proved successful, and the tower has survived intact for more than a hundred years. Its third-order flashing light intended to warn ships away from shoals off Cape San Blas was discontinued in 1996 when the station was deactivated.

TO SEE THE LIGHT: Located about half a mile from a U.S. Air Force radar station, the lighthouse is not open to the public, but visitors are welcome to walk the grounds. The area can be reached via Highways 30 and 30E.

Location: Cape San Blas

Established: 1848

Tower height: 90 feet

Elevation of the focal plane: 90 feet

Optic: Fresnel lens (third order) still in place

Status: Deactivated in 1996

Note: Lighthouses here have been repeatedly destroyed and rebuilt

The open-walled, iron-skeleton structure of the existing Cape San Blas Lighthouse tower offers little resistance to wind, and so helps protect the lighthouse from storms.

ST. JOSEPH BAY LIGHTHOUSE

I n 1838 delegates gathered in what was then
the thriving Gulf port of St. Joseph to frame
Florida's first state constitution. That same year
the federal government acknowledged the town's
growing importance by placing a lighthouse on
the far tip of the St. Joseph peninsula to guide
ships into St. Joseph Bay. Neither the town nor
the lighthouse would last, however. A yellow fever
epidemic severely depopulated the entire region,
and then the tower and the town sank in the flood
tides of a titanic gale that hit the area in 1847.

From the ruins of the once-thriving community of
St. Joseph, the village of Port St. Joe emerged,
but more than half a century passed before the
government thought it merited a lighthouse. Finally,
in 1903, a square, wooden combination dwelling
and tower was built on the mainland, directly
across from St. Joseph Point. The lantern, situated
atop the peaked roof of the main building, held a
third-order Fresnel lens.

In 1960 the Coast Guard closed the St. Joseph
Bay station, replacing its light with an automated
beacon displayed from atop a steel tower resem-
bling a broadcast antenna. The old lighthouse was
sold off for use as a barn. Several years ago it was
purchased and refurbished as a private residence.

TO SEE THE LIGHT: From Port St. Joe drive northwest for 10 miles to Beacon Hill. The existing steel
tower rises just to the west of Beacon Road. The
site of the original station is nearby.

Location: Port St. Joe

Established: 1838

Tower height: 55 feet

Status: Removed

Note: Yellow fever
epidemic reduced need
for the light

Passersby might never guess this handsome coastal residence was
once a lighthouse. For many years, after it was retired from active
service, the St. Joseph Bay Lighthouse was used as a barn.
Bob and Sandra Shanklin, The Lighthouse People

PENSACOLA LIGHT

Following the acquisition of Florida from Spain in 1821, President James Monroe ordered the U.S. Navy into the Gulf of Mexico to flush out pirates. With no base on the Gulf Coast, the U.S. fleet might as well have been patrolling foreign waters. Then the navy found exactly what it needed at Pensacola: a deep-water port for its fighting ships. To this day, the U.S. Navy maintains a significant presence at Pensacola.

To guide navy warships in and out of the new base, the U.S. Lighthouse Service established a station in Pensacola in 1824. Winslow Lewis built the 45-foot tower on a sandy spit near the entrance to the harbor, fitting it with oil lamps and reflectors of his own design. Lewis billed the government a modest $5,725 for the entire project. Even so, the station was not worth its cost, for like many Lewis beacons, this one proved far less than adequate. Its light was so weak that captains often ran their ships aground while searching for it.

In 1858 a 171-foot-tall brick tower replaced the old Lewis lighthouse. It cost nearly $46,000, a bargain considering the tower has survived hurricanes, lightning strikes, and more than 140 years' worth of wear and tear, not to mention a fierce Union cannonade during the Civil War. Moreover, its impressive height and first-order Fresnel lens more than doubled the range of the old Lewis beacon to better than 25 miles. Now automated, the old light still guides navy ships and Coast Guard cutters in and out of the harbor.

TO SEE THE LIGHT: Follow Navy Boulevard (Highway 295) to the Pensacola Naval Air Station. The guard at the gate can provide a car pass and directions to the lighthouse. Exhibits at the nearby Naval Air Museum celebrate the history of the light station and the U.S. Navy's strong links to Pensacola; for additional information call the museum at (850) 452–3604.

Location: Pensacola

Established: 1824

Tower height: 171 feet

Elevation of the focal plane: 191 feet

Optic: Fresnel lens (first order)

Status: Active

Characteristic: Flashes every 20 seconds

Range: 27 miles

Position: 30° 20' 28 87° 18' 30

Note: Among the tallest light towers in the United States

GLOSSARY

Argand lamp

A clean-burning oil lamp widely used in lighthouses during the late eighteenth and early nineteenth centuries. Designed by French inventor Ami Argand, they produced an intense flame and a very bright light.

Automated light

A lighthouse with no keeper. Following World War II, remote-control systems, light-activated switches, and fog-sensing devices made automation an increasingly cost-effective and attractive option, and the efficiency-minded Coast Guard automated one light station after another. By 1970 only about sixty lighthouses still had full-time keepers, and within two decades all but one of those beacons had been automated. All of Florida's active lighthouses are now automated.

Beacon

A light or radio signal intended to guide mariners or aviators.

Caisson towers

During the late nineteenth century, the government began building offshore lighthouses on caissons. Essentially, a caisson was a hollow shell made of heavy, rolled-iron plates. Bolted together on land, the caisson was hauled to the construction site, sunk into the seabed up to a depth of about 30 feet, and then filled with sand, gravel, rock, or concrete. Completed in 1872, the Duxbury Lighthouse near Plymouth, Massachusetts, is said to be the oldest caisson tower in the United States.

Cast-iron towers

Introduced as a building material during the 1840s, cast iron revolutionized lighthouse construction. Stronger than stone and relatively light, cast iron made it possible to fabricate parts of a light tower in a far-off foundry and then ship them to the construction site for assembly. A cylindrical structure assembled in 1844 on Long Island Head in Boston Harbor may have been the first all-cast-iron lighthouse.

Characteristic

The identifying feature of a lighthouse beacon. To help mariners tell one beacon from another, maritime officials give each light a distinct color or pattern of flashes. Among the more famous lighthouse characteristics is that of the offshore Minots Ledge Light near Scituate, Massachusetts, which displays a single flash, followed by four quick flashes, then three more. This one-four-three flashing sequence reminds some romantic observers of I-LOVE-YOU.

Clamshell or bivalve lenses

Most Fresnel lenses are round, but some have a slightly squeezed or flattened shape somewhat like that of a clamshell. They nearly always feature a pair of bull's-eyes or focal points, one on each side of the lens.

Clockwork mechanism

Early rotating lighthouse lenses were often driven by a set of gears, weights, and pulleys similar to those used in large clocks. Every few hours the keeper had to "rewind" the machinery by pulling or cranking the weights to the top of the tower.

Coast Guard, U.S.

Since 1939, lighthouses and other aids to navigation in the United States have been the responsibility of the U.S. Coast Guard. Previously, the nation's maritime lights were maintained by a separate government agency known as the U.S. Lighthouse Service.

Cottage style

Consisting of a small, single-story wooden building with a light tower and lantern on the roof, cottage-style lighthouses were once quite common, especially in the bays and inlets of the American south. Combining the keeper's quarters, workrooms, and tower kept construction costs quite low and made these modest light stations relatively easy to maintain. Often octagonal or hexagonal in shape, they usually stood on piles in open water.

Daymark

An unlighted maritime marker useful only during daylight hours. Sometimes abandoned light towers are left standing so they can continue to serve mariners as daymarks.

Elevation or height of the focal plane

Fresnel lenses and most modern optical systems channel light signals into a narrow band known as the focal plane. Since the curvature of the earth would render low-lying lights practically worthless for navigation, a coastal beacon must have an elevated focal plane. The height of the plane above the water's surface— usually from 40 to 200 feet—helps determine the range of the light.

Fixed signal

A lighthouse beacon that shines constantly during its regular hours of operation is said to display a "fixed" signal.

Flashing signal

A lighthouse beacon that turns on and off or grows much brighter at regular intervals is called a flashing signal.

Focal plane

See Elevation or height of the focal plane

Fog signal or foghorn

A distinct sound signal, usually a horn, trumpet, or siren, used to warn vessels away from prominent headlands or navigational obstacles during fog or other periods of low visibility.

Fresnel lenses

Invented in 1822 by Augustin Fresnel, a noted French physicist, Fresnel lenses concentrate light into a powerful beam that can be seen over great distances. Usually, they consist of individual hand-polished glass prisms arrayed in a bronze frame. Manufactured by a number of French and British companies, these devices came in as many as eleven different sizes or "orders." A massive first-order lens may be more than 6 feet in diameter and 12 feet tall, while a diminutive sixth-order lens is only about 1 foot wide and not much larger than an ordinary gallon jug.

Gallery

A circular walkway with a railing around the lantern of a lighthouse. Galleries provided keepers convenient access to the outside of the lantern for window cleaning, painting, and repair work.

Harbor light

A beacon intended to assist vessels moving in and out of a harbor. Not meant to serve as major coastal markers, harbor lights often consisted of little more than a lantern hung from a pole. However, many were official light stations with a tower and residence for the keeper.

Keeper

Before the era of automation, responsibility for operating and maintaining a light station was placed in the hands of a keeper, sometimes aided by one or more assistants. During the eighteenth and nineteenth centuries keepers were appointed by the Treasury Department or even the president himself in return for military service or a political favor. Although the work was hard and the pay minimal, these appointments were coveted since they offered a steady income and free housing.

Keeper's residence or dwelling

The presence of a keeper's residence is what turned a light station into a light "house." Sometime keepers lived in the tower itself, but a typical lighthouse dwelling was a detached one-and-a-half-story wood or stone structure built in a style similar to that of other working-class homes in the area.

Lamp and reflector

For several decades prior to the introduction of the highly efficient Fresnel lens, lighthouse beacons were intensified by means of lamp-and-reflector systems. These combined a bright-burning lamp and a polished mirror shaped in a manner intended to concentrate the light.

Lantern

The glass-enclosed space at the top of a light tower. It houses the lens or optic and protects it from the weather.

Lewis, Isaiah (I. W. P.)

A mid-nineteenth century civil engineer and lighthouse inspector, Lewis advocated construction of iron-skeleton light towers such as the failed Minots Ledge Light tower off Cohasset, Massachusetts, and the more durable Carysfort Reef Light in the Florida Keys. Lewis was a vociferous critic of his uncle, the noted lighthouse contractor Winslow Lewis.

Lewis, Winslow

A former New England sea captain, Winslow Lewis built dozens of U.S. lighthouses during the first half of the nineteenth century. Lewis introduced his own version of the Argand lamp-and-reflector system, which most people considered vastly inferior to the original.

Light station

A navigational facility with a light beacon. Often the term is used interchangeably with "lighthouse," but a light station may or may not include a tower, quarters for a keeper, or a fog signal.

Light tower

A tall, often cylindrical, structure used to elevate a navigational light so that mariners can see it from a distance. Modern light towers support a lantern, which houses a lamp, electric beacon, or some other lighting device. Some light towers are an integral part of the station residence but most are detached.

Lighthouse

A term applied to a wide variety of buildings constructed for the purpose of guiding ships. Often it is used interchangeably with similar or derivative terms such as "light tower" or "light station." Throughout this book you will often find the more general term "light" used in reference to individual lighthouses or light stations where the beacon remains in operation.

Lighthouse Board

Beginning in 1851 and for more than half a century afterward, U.S. lighthouses were administered by the U.S. Lighthouse Board, which consisted of nine members. Usually board members were noted engineers, scientists, or military men. Creation of the board brought a professional spirit and penchant for innovation to the Lighthouse Service. Perhaps the board's most significant contribution was its adoption of the advanced Fresnel lens as the standard U.S. lighthouse optic.

Lighthouse Service

A common term applied to the various organizations or agencies that built and maintained U.S. lighthouses from 1789 until 1939 when the Coast Guard was placed in charge.

Lightships

Equipped with their own beacons, usually displayed from a tall, central mast, lightships were essentially floating lighthouses. They marked shoals or key navigational turning points where construction of a permanent light tower was either impossible or prohibitively expensive.

Meade, George

Meade is best known as the Civil War general who led the Union to victory at Gettysburg, but before the war he was an army engineer specializing in lighthouse construction. Meade's innovative designs greatly increased the durability of open-water towers. His iron-skeleton towers in the Florida Keys still stand and continue to serve mariners more than 150 years after they were built.

Modern optic

A term referring to a broad array of lightweight, mostly weatherproof, devices that produce the most modern navigational lights.

Occulting or eclipsing light

There are several ways to produce a beacon that appears to flash. One is to "occult" or block the light at regular intervals, often with a rotating opaque panel.

Private aid to navigation

A privately owned and maintained navigational light. Often, such lights are formerly deactivated beacons that have been reestablished for historic or aesthetic purposes.

Range lights

Displayed in pairs, range lights help mariners keep their vessels safely within the narrow navigable channels that criss-cross estuaries or lead in and out of harbors. The rear-range light is higher and farther from the water than its partner, the front-range light, which is often located at water's edge. When viewed from mid-channel, the lights appear in perfect vertical alignment.

Red sector

Some lighthouses display a multicolored beacon. For instance, an otherwise white beacon may appear red to mariners approaching a dangerous obstacle. Such navigational lights are said to have a "red sector."

Screw-pile towers

Open-water lighthouses built in rivers, bays, and other shallow water areas were often placed on piles that had been fitted with spiral flanges that made it possible to screw them into the subsurface sedimentary material. The screw piles often supported a lightweight wooden cottage with a small tower and lantern on its roof.

Skeleton towers

Iron- or steel-skeleton light towers consist of four or more heavily braced metal legs topped by workrooms and/or a lantern. Relatively durable and inexpensive, they were built in considerable numbers during the latter half of the nineteenth century. Since their open walls offer little resistance to wind and water, these towers proved ideal for offshore navigational stations.

Solar-powered optic

Nowadays, many remote lighthouse beacons are powered by batteries recharged during the day by solar panels.

Spark plug, teakettle, or coffeepot lights

Many open-water lighthouses in northern climates are built on round, concrete-filled caissons, which protect them from fast-flowing water and ice floes. Usually the massive caissons are black while the cylindrical iron towers on top of them are painted white, giving them the appearance of an automobile spark plug. However, some think they look more like teakettles or coffeepots.

Twin light

A few lighthouses once exhibited two separate lights. This was done to distinguish the beacon from other prominent nearby lights.

ABOUT THE AUTHORS

Photographs by **Bruce Roberts** have appeared in numerous magazines, including *Life* and *Sports Illustrated*, and in hundreds of books, many of them about lighthouses. He was director of photography at *Southern Living* magazine for many years. His work is also on display in the permanent collection at the Smithsonian Institution. He lives in Morehead City, North Carolina.

Ray Jones is the author or coauthor of fourteen best-selling books about lighthouses. He has served as an editor at Time-Life Books, as founding editor of *Albuquerque Living* magazine, as writing coach at *Southern Living* magazine, and as founding publisher of Country Roads Press. He lives in Pebble Beach, California, where he continues to write about lighthouses and serves as a consultant to businesses, publishers, and other authors.

ALSO BY BRUCE ROBERTS AND RAY JONES

Lighthouses of Massachusetts
A Guidebook and Keepsake

Lighthouses of California
A Guidebook and Keepsake

Lighthouses of Michigan
A Guidebook and Keepsake

New England Lighthouses
Maine to Long Island Sound

American Lighthouses
A Comprehensive Guide

Eastern Great Lakes Lighthouses
Ontario, Erie, and Huron

Western Great Lakes Lighthouses
Michigan and Superior

Gulf Coast Lighthouses
Florida Keys to the Rio Grande

Mid-Atlantic Coast Lighthouses
Hudson River to Chesapeake Bay

Pacific Northwest Lighthouses
Oregon, Washington, Alaska, and British Columbia

Southern Lighthouses
Outer Banks to Cape Florida